LOVER OF THE WILDERNESS

Life and Teaching of Father Pimen
of the Monastery of the Syrians

H.G. BISHOP DOMATIUS

Lover of the Wilderness: Life and Teaching of Father Pimen of the Monastery of the Syrians
By H.G. Bishop Domatius

Copyright © 2023 Coptic Orthodox Diocese of the Southern U.S.A.

All rights reserved.

Designed & Published by:
St. Mary & St. Moses Abbey Press
101 S Vista Dr, Sandia, TX 78383
stmabbeypress.com

Translation from Arabic by St. Mary & St. Moses Abbey.

All Scripture quotations in the footnotes of this book, unless otherwise indicated, are taken from the New King James Version® Copyright © 1982 by Thomas Nelson, Inc. Used by permission. All rights reserved. The rest of the quotations in this book are derived directly from St. John Chrysostom, who is known to have relied on the Septuagint and other early manuscripts available to him.

Contents

Forward	V
Introduction	VII

PART ONE: FATHER PIMEN'S LIFE

Chapter 1: His Birth and Early Life	11
Chapter 2: His Monastic Life	45
Chapter 3: His Spiritual Virtues	78
Chapter 4 His Relationship with the Saints	102
Chapter 5: Ocurrences and Wonders	120
Chapter 6: His Last Illness and Departure	131

PART TWO: FATHER PIMEN'S TEACHING

Chapter 1: His Monastic Principles	149
Chapter 2: His Spiritual Meditations	158
Chapter 3: His Spiritual Sayings	196
Chapter 4: A Dialogue with Fr. Pimen	203

Forward

In the Name of the Father and the Son and the Holy Spirit, One God. Amen.

A whole year has passed quickly on the departure of the blessed father, the monk Pimen[1].

He was a great monk, an ardent lover of the wilderness, a good role model for the monks, a teacher of generations, who was long-suffering, patient, giving thanks to God in the most difficult conditions of his illness.

The reverend father, the monk Hegumen Zachariah of the Syrians,[2] with the help of some of the monks of the monastery, began collecting and categorizing the material for this book about the monk Hegumen Pimen, on the occasion of a year passing on his departure.

Written in this book is valuable information about his upbringing, childhood and his early youth; about his service in Sunday School and youth meetings in Qalyub and the rest of Egypt; about his torrential longing for monasticism; about his entering the monastery and his tonsuring as a monk on November 5, 1972. Also written is information about the service he offered the monks and his care for their health as a doctor; about his monastic strivings and his solitude in his solitary cell in the garden of the monastery; about the [spiritual] service he offered the monks and his meetings with them to explain Biblical passages, being an educated person who has gone into the depth; about his sermons and his spiritual sittings and his conversations with some of the monks. Finally, this book includes information about

---

1   Pimen Al-Souriany.
2   Now: His Grace Bishop Domatius, Bishop of Sixth of October, Ousim and its territories, Giza, Egypt.

his last illness and his long-suffering with thanksgiving until his departure on November 5, 2010, which is the [exact] day of his tonsuring, after spending 38 whole years in monasticism, which was fruitful and profitable for the monastery and his eternal life.

I leave you, my dear reader, with this profitable book, that you may read in it many words of benefit said by Fr. Pimen, whether in his sermons or his sittings with the monks of the monastery, and that you may learn from him patience and thanksgiving in all circumstances of life. As our teacher James the Apostle said, "But let patience have its perfect work, that you may be perfect and complete, lacking nothing."[3] And as our teacher Paul the Apostle said, "If we endure, we shall also reign with Him."[4]

May God grant us the heavenly inheritance with Fr. Pimen and all the saints who have pleased God by their good works, through the intercessions of the Lady of us all and the pride of our race, the pure Saint Mary, and through the prayers of our blessed father, the honorable Pope Shenouda III. To our God be all glory and honor forever. Amen.

Bishop Mettaos
Abbot of the monastery of the Syrians

---

[3] James 1:4.
[4] 2 Timothy 2:12.

Introduction

"I wonder whether the sky with all its stars is more luminous than the Wilderness of Scetis with its monks." This is how St. John Chrysostom described the monks of the Wilderness of Scetis, that they shone like stars, out of their great purity and their holy fellowship with God. One of these shining stars adorning the Wilderness of Scetis in our current generation is Fr. Pimen, who through his spiritual strivings, his numerous virtues, his pure teachings, and through fleeing the vainglories of the world, has become worthy of shining crowns of glory in the heavens.

The fragrant life of Fr. Pimen is a good role model for every soul aspiring to acquire Christian virtues, and it is encouraging also to everyone desirous of leaving the vainglories of the world and walking onward after the Lord Christ.

The life of Fr. Pimen reminds us of the lives of the saintly fathers of the early centuries of monasticism, like the Sts. Maximus and Dometius, and the saint Abba Arsenius the teacher of the Emperor's sons, St. Hilary the daughter of Emperor Zeno, and others who have renounced the passing, worldly positions and walked carrying their cross behind the Lord Christ, that they may receive the glories of the Resurrection with Him.

The coming generations will envy us on seeing this virtuous father, with whom we lived and to whose teachings and guidance we enjoyed listening, which were encouraging and directive for every fainting soul walking in the spiritual path.

Our father Pimen lived the life of unceasing prayer while still on earth, remembering his children the monks and praying for their salvation. Therefore we have confidence also that in heaven, he will not cease to pray for them always before the throne of grace.[5]

I would like to extend the most bounteous thanks to His Grace Bishop Mettaos, Bishop and Abbot of the monastery of the Syrians, who is a lover of the biographies of contemporary fathers and who encourages publishing them, who took much of his time to review this book and to write an introduction for it. I would like also to offer my sincere thanks to Dr. Youssef Ameen, Fr. Pimen's youngest brother, all his sisters and their children, and all who loved him, who provided us information about him. Also, I would like to offer thanks to my fathers the monks of the monastery of the Syrians, especially thanking his children the monks and novices who served him and took care of him during his illness, as they gave us much information and helped us in releasing this book as is fitting of this virtuous father and venerable elder. I would like not to miss offering thanks to all who contributed and participated in covering the cost and in printing this book. May the Lord recompense all with the heavenly reward. We ask the Lord to let His Holy Spirit work in the heart of every reader of this fragrant biography.

Through the prayers and supplications which the Mother of God, the pure Virgin, St. Mary offers for us always, and the prayers of His Holiness, the honorable Pope Shenouda III, and his partner in the apostolic liturgy, our honorable father Bishop Mettaos, Bishop and Abbot of the monastery of the Syrians, and the prayers of our father Pimen. To our God be the glory in His holy Church. Amen.

Bishop Domatius
Bishop of Sixth of October, Ousim and its territories, Giza, Egypt

---

5   See Hebrews 4:16.

PART ONE

Father Pimen's Life

CHAPTER ONE

His Birth and Early Life

The Nobility of His Ancestry

> "Before I formed you in the womb I knew you;
> before you were born I sanctified you; I ordained
> you a prophet to the nations."[6]

Fr. Pimen[7] came from a house descending from a priestly family that dwelt in the city of Luxor. He had seven ancestors who were priests, the greatest of whom was Hegumen Hanna Gabriel Ekladios who was the first priest to travel to Sudan to open its churches and pray therein after the Mahdy revolution which closed all the churches of Sudan. Hegumen Hanna is the latest hegumen in this family, whose tomb is currently in the city of Luxor, visited by people for blessing. Dr. Wadih Ameen (Fr. Pimen) visited it after he graduated from medical school and was employed as a physician in the city of Luxor, where he was accompanied by Hegumen Abdel Messih of Luxor, to see it and take his blessing. As they were standing beside the shrine, Hegumen Abdel Messih related to him some miracles that occurred through the relics of his grandfather Hegumen Hanna Gabriel Ekladios.

His Birth and Upbringing

> "And you will have joy and gladness, and many
> will rejoice at his birth. For he will be great in the
> sight of the LORD."[8]

Mr. Ameen Nabeeh Khalil Heg. Hanna was brought up in the city of Luxor in Upper Egypt. He was one of the members of the family of the previously mentioned Hegumen Gabriel Ekladios. He was a righteous and godly man, of whose righteousness the men of his town

---

6   Jeremiah 1:5.
7   Fr. Pimen Al-Souriany, that is, of the monastery of the Syrians.
8   Luke 1:14–15.

testified. His employment happened to be in the city of Qalyub Elbalad, where God gave him a virtuous wife named Nazeima Youssef Soliman, and they lived together a good life in the fear of God and His love, until their report spread, and their good manner of life became the talk of everyone in town. As the Holy Scripture testified of Zacharias and Elizabeth, that "they were both righteous before God, walking in all the commandments and ordinances of the Lord blameless,"[9] so did God testify of their righteousness. He blessed them and gave them two sons (Wadih and Youssef) and three daughters (Afifa, Anjeel and Amal).

The birth of their son Wadih was on Sunday December 8, 1929, in Qalyub Elbalad in the Qalyubia governorate. This was the cause of a great joy for his parents, for he was [their] first son after his sister Afifa.

The five siblings grew up in the life of godliness and faith which their parents, who brought them up with sound spiritual and physical care, instilled in them. Both of them encouraged [their children] to pray, to go to church and to partake of the Holy Mysteries every week, besides teaching them love, almsgiving and mercy. Their mother had two aunts, one a widow who had no children, while the second had vowed to be a bride for Christ. These two sisters lived together in a house [located] across from the house of Mr. Ameen's family. Their whole life was fasting, prayer, almsgiving

---

9   Luke 1:6.

and holiness. From time to time, these sisters would help their niece in caring for her children. Therefore, these children soaked up from them a life of godliness, holiness, and Christian faith.

A Strange Visitor and a Marvelous Thing

> "Behold, I stand at the door and knock. If anyone hears My voice and opens the door, I will come in to him and dine with him, and he with Me."[10]

Before the child Wadih was two years in age, it happened one day that while he was in his aunts' house, and the door of the house was open, his maiden aunt saw a man standing outside the door. He was wearing a long shoddy garment[11]. At first glance, he looked like one of the poor coming to ask for alms, so she went to him and asked him about what he needed. However, he was silent and said not a word to her; rather, he grabbed the fringe of his garment with his hand and began flapping with it. She figured that he wanted to get from her a new garment to wear. So she said to him, "Sir, we do not have any clothes that may be of use to you, for we are two women living in this house, but wait a little. Maybe I could find something for you." The woman walked away for a moment and brought a white garment and offered it to him. After he took it from her, he disappeared immediately from before her. She hurried after him towards the street, while crying out, that maybe she could catch him, but she came back to her house disappointed as she could find no trace of him. Here, the aunt of the child Wadih realized, after returning to her house, that this man who came to her

---

10   Revelations 3:20.
11   Such a garment is known in Arabic as *gallabiyah*. It is a long loose garment or tunic worn by laymen in some parts of Egypt. Monks and priests wear black *gallabiyah*.

house was [either] the Lord Jesus or one of the saints. Therefore, she began sweeping the place where the man had stepped upon with his feet, and collected it in a bag. She put some of it on the child Wadih's head of and rubbed his body with it, for she had strong faith that if she did this to the child Wadih, his sick feet, which he had difficulty walking on, would be healed. After this strange incident took place and after what the aunt did, the child Wadih began to walk and move normally.

A Small Child... I Wonder Who He Might Be?

> "Now as they said these things, Jesus Himself stood in the midst of them, and said to them, 'Peace to you'... And He took it and ate in their presence."[12]

After a year had passed on what had happened to the child Wadih in his aunt's home, being three years old at this time, something happened which was even stranger than what had happened before, but this time in his father's home. The child Wadih was in the house with his mother alone; the house's door was closed in fear that her little child would leave the house unnoticed and any harm would befall him. Wanting to keep her child Wadih busy with anything, so that she may do [some] housework, she brought him a plate of pudding, gave him a spoon, and left him eating, until she would have finished her housework. And from time to time, she would come back to check on him. After five minutes had passed, the mother came back to her son to find a small child his age sitting beside him, and he would stretch out his hand into the plate with [her son] and eat with his finger. So the mother asked the child saying, "Who are you my son? Should I bring another plate for you to eat?" She played with the child and patted him

---

12   Luke 24:36, 43.

on his shoulder, and at that [moment], she noticed that she had closed the door of her house a short while ago. She was troubled and said to the child, "How did you get in and where did you come from, the door being closed?" When she said this to the child, he disappeared immediately and she could not find a trace of him in the house. When she saw what had happened, she marveled and began thinking to herself, "I wonder who this child might be."

A Dove Resting[13] Upon the Chalice

> "And immediately coming up from the water, He saw the heavens parting and the Spirit descending upon Him like a dove."[14]

The godly mother was accustomed to taking her children to church with her every week, and at the time, her son Wadih was five years old. As he was standing beside her quietly, he suddenly started to stir, look at his mother, and push her with his hands, and when she did not give him attention, he cried out, saying, "Mom! Mom! A dove is resting on the chalice. Hurry up! Tell the priest." This was at the time of the Prayer of the Descent of the Holy Spirit in the Liturgy.

The mother then realized what her son Wadih had seen and began calming him down. She kept all these things in her heart, and at the end of the Liturgy, the mother and her little son met the priest, and she told him about all that her son Wadih had seen. The priest blessed him and marveled at the innocence and purity of the heart of the child Wadih which made him worthy to see the Holy Spirit descending upon the Mysteries in the form of a dove.

---

13   Literally: standing.
14   Mark 1:10.

Harsh Orders and a Merciful Kiss

> "And that from childhood you have known the Holy Scriptures, which are able to make you wise for salvation through faith which is in Christ Jesus."[15]

The child Wadih joined the Dutch Missionary School in Qalyub Elbalad, and signs of geniality and intelligence were clearly manifest in him from young age. It was clear that he excelled well beyond the students in the classroom. And at this early age, he manifested a tendency towards much reading, besides his attributes of calmness and meekness. He was therefore loved by his fellow students, teachers and all who interacted with him.

It happened one day, when Wadih was in the second grade of elementary [school], that the Arabic language teacher was giving a lesson in syntax to the fourth grade class. The teacher asked one of the students to parse a word. When the fourth grader failed to give the correct answer, the teacher scolded him and rebuked him severely for not knowing, and said to him, "Had I asked a second grader this question, he would have answered it correctly." And indeed the teacher went to the second grade classroom, picked the student Wadih and asked him the same question, to which he gave the correct answer. This so gladdened the teacher's heart that he began thanking the student Wadih and asked him, in the end, to slap the fourth grader on the cheek, because of the latter's failure to answer correctly. The child Wadih hesitated initially and did not move, but when the teacher sternly repeated the order, Wadih stepped forward, put both of his hands on the fourth grader's face, and instead of slapping him, he kissed him on his

---

15 2 Timothy 3:15.

cheek, amidst the clapping of the students and their joy in him. What Wadih did was a source of admiration of the teachers and students, for his [great] wisdom despite his young age.

The First Seeds of Monasticism

> "But others fell on good ground and yielded a crop."[16]

The nature of the youth Wadih tended toward calmness, stillness, and avoidance of much mingling with those his age. These traits cultivated in him a love of reading of any book that fell into his hands, especially spiritual books, and he read them with passion like someone devouring delicious food. Here, we keep silent so that we may hear Fr. Pimen telling us about the first book he read; his reverence says:

> I loved monasticism since I was 13 years old, and the first book I read was, Taming the Minds in the Paradise of the Monks by Hegumen Armanius Habashi El-Baramawy. I became attached to this book and I loved it a lot, for it was the first monastic seed that fell onto my heart and therein kindled the fire of Divine love.

Spiritual Activity and Early Service

> "...And [He] taught. And they were astonished at His teaching, for he taught them as one having authority, and not as the scribes."[17]

In that early stage of his life, the youth Wadih grew

---

16   Matthew 13:8.
17   Mark 1:21–22.

noticeably in his spiritual zeal and his attachment to the church. While still being 13 years old, he started a visitation service for the children of St. George's church in Qalyub, and he would give them Sunday
School lessons. As time went by, an overflowing love was kindled in him toward the people he served, and these same feelings they held for him in return. When Wadih became an adolescent in high school, he was able to move around here and there, and an opportunity permitted him to be introduced to the Sunday School [servants] in Giza, who helped and assisted him with many things concerning the service: [for example, he was given] a device that displays movies (projector) and photos. He would use these means in the youth meetings he organized, or in the periodical parties and religious plays in which the children and youth performed.

He also organized hymns classes until a big chorus was formed in the church. They sang the church hymns so wonderfully that they won the admiration of the congregation. When the people of the nearby towns and villages heard of this activity, they would initially come to Qalyub to watch Christian movies and religious plays and to listen to sermons. Afterwards, the young man Wadih prepared some servants to go to these towns and villages, to give them Sunday School lessons. He used to sit with them and teach them how to give sermons to the people and children, which made the people in these villages marvel at these young boys, at their ability in giving sermons.

The range of the service expanded to the extent of

holding conferences for Sunday School, which were attended by prominent servants in these regions. Of these was the great servant Nazir Gayed Raphael (H.H. Pope Shenouda III—may God prolong his life); and Hegumen Saleeb Sorial from Giza; and Mr. Maleka Eskander from Shabeen El-Kanater who became afterwards Hegumen Mina Eskander in Alexandria; and many [other] servants besides those mentioned.

Thunderous Outcries of a Bold Young Man

"Zeal for your house has eaten Me up."[18]

The young man Wadih joined the Major Coptic High School near the Patriarchate in Azbakeya. It happened on one of those days, while he was in school, that he heard the news of the burning of a church in Suez City, so zeal and ardor seized him and he was transformed into another person. He moved with excitement and anger among the students' classrooms in the courtyard of the school, crying out in a loud voice, condemning the burning of the Suez church. From a cry to another, he would repeat, "Live Pope Macarius!" [That] school day ended in thunderous cries, after he joined many Christian students in the region, amidst the amazement of the teachers, who marveled at the courage and boldness of the student Wadih.

Answering in Wisdom

"And all who heard Him were astonished at His understanding and answers."[19]

While the student Wadih Ameen was in the Major Coptic High School in Azbakeya listening to the lecture of one

---
18 John 2:17.
19 Luke 2:47.

of the teachers in the classroom, the teacher strayed from the lesson and began inquiring tauntingly about the verse that says, "But whoever slaps you on your right cheek, turn the other to him also."[20] He deprecated the verse and attacked it saying that these words were not reasonable nor logical, because they make people persist in their assaulting [others]. As the teacher overstepped [his boundaries] and taunted, Wadih raised his hand and stood before the teacher saying that this commandment is not for an individual or particular individuals [only] but it is for all people, so if all performed it, there would not be a person hitting nor another hit. Wadih stood still as the teacher was silent before this confuting answer. He looked astounded, not knowing what to do, [but finally] said to him, defeated, "Sit down, you philosopher!" Wadih then sat down in his place and all the students who heard him were astonished at his understanding and answers.

Caring About His Own Salvation

> "Take heed to yourself and to the doctrine. Continue in them, for in doing this you will save both yourself and those who hear you."[21]

The great, wide activity the young man Wadih did in Sunday School service was not done to the detriment of his spiritual life. Rather, his activity in the service invigorated him in the spiritual struggle; his ardor and zeal for the salvation of the souls whom he served increased his zeal and heed to his own salvation. Therefore, he was meticulous in his prayers, his psalms, and reading the Holy Bible, and in his fasts and precise confession. He was also meticulous in his conduct and

---

20 Matthew 5:39.
21 1 Timothy 4:16.

his purity, following the words of Paul the Apostle to his disciple Timothy, "Be an example to the believers in word, in conduct, in love, in spirit, in faith, in purity."[22] Here we leave the conversation to Fr. Pimen to tell us about his meticulousness, his commitment, and his earnestness in his spiritual life when he was a young man. So his reverence says:

Fr. Hanna Kamel of St. Macarius[23] was my first father of confession. I used to go to him regularly with some young men for confession. He was so strict with us in our confession to him, that if he found out that one of us was not consistent in his psalms and prayers, he would prevent him from [receiving] communion. And this strictness with which Hegumen Hanna of St. Macarius dealt with us taught us commitment and faithfulness in our spiritual life.

Surviving a Terrible Accident

"Behold the eye of the LORD is on those who fear Him, on those who hope in His mercy, to deliver their soul from death."[24]

One day, after finishing his school day, Dr. Wadih Ameen left Kasr Al-Ainy Medical School, heading toward the railroad station to take the train back to Qalyub. When he arrived at the station, he found that the train was [just] starting to move away from the platform, so he ran quickly after it so that he may catch the last car. With great difficulty, he was able to catch the door handle with his hand, but when he tried to put his feet inside the train car, he missed his target in putting them inside and his feet fell between the platform and the

---

22　1 Timothy 4:12.
23　In Arabic: Al-Makari.
24　Psalms 33:18–19.

train. He lost control, falling onto the platform, on which the moving train dragged him. And before the train left the platform, Dr. Wadih heard a voice behind him, which said to him, "Leave the door handle, I am holding you." In faith and trust, Dr. Wadih let go of the door handle and found himself on the platform. When the train had left [the station], he began inspecting his body for possibly a wound or fracture, but he found no harm nor injury, no trace of a cut, nor [even] his clothes getting dirty. He then turned around, to look for the person whose voice he heard behind him, to thank him, but he found nobody at all. Here, he remembered the psalm that says, "The angel of the Lord encamps all around those who fear Him, and delivers them."[25] At that moment, he realized that it was the voice of his guardian angel, which he heard behind him, whom God had sent to save him from a sure death.

His Graduation and His Work as a Physician

> "Let your light so shine before men that they may see your good works and glorify your Father in heaven."[26]

Dr. Wadih Ameen completed his studies successfully, with excellence, and received a bachelor's [degree] from the Faculty of Medicine Kasr Al-Ainy[27] Department of Surgery. His success and excellence in his studies are due to his success in his spiritual life, and his service as well. In his brilliant success, Dr. Wadih had given an honorable image for the children of God, and a good role model to be imitated by all who aspire to success.

Dr. Wadih worked as a physician in many places. His

---

25 Psalms 34:7.
26 Matthew 5:16.
27 Cairo University.

first appointment as a physician was in the city of Luxor, the city of his ancestors. He then moved to Marsa Matroh, and afterwards to Borj Al-Arab. It was in the latter, where he became an intimate friend with Major General Mohamed Naguib, who was one of the Free Officers[28] who led the 1952 revolution, and afterwards became the first president of the government [of Egypt].  There were between them numerous correspondences. We place before our dear reader one of these letters sent by Major General Mohamed Naguib, which revealed to us many things in the life of Dr. Wadih Ameen. In this letter, he commends him for his concern and care for the poor, saying to him, "The Lord may support you, and make of you always a most impregnable fortress for humanity and a benefactor of the poor." He continues his commendation also, and says, "Furthermore, I have received your letter... And I have been trying to answer it by coming to you personally at the hospital, to thank you for your exemplary humanity." And after he presented, in many words, the obstacles that prevented his coming, he also commends him, saying, "I hastened to compose this to you, that I may thank you greatly, for I love each person who sympathizes with the children of his nation, whenever the latter were poor or in need of care." Though Major General Mohamed Naguib [sent] this magnitude of appreciation and thanks to Dr. Wadih, he did not stop at that but he continued, on every line or two, to commend and thank him. He wrote to him, saying, "I felt a great happiness for what this unfortunate[29] [woman] has received; your exceedingly

---

28 Member of the Free Officers Movement.
29 Literally: miserable.

great care and your merciful heart. For it is rare for people like her to be met whole-heartedly, and often they do not get a tenth of a tenth of your care, except rarely. I had prayed and asked the Lord Almighty to take care of her, so He prepared for her a man with a big heart like you."

In the end he says, "I will strive, in the first opportunity, to visit your lordship, so that I may attain to seeing a man, [who is] noble, great, having precious morals..." Undoubtedly, this wonderful letter which Major General Mohamed Naguib wrote to Dr. Wadih Ameen, has spared us, dear reader, from [trying to] illustrate to you the personality of Dr. Wadih and his work as a physician, after he revealed to us what we were incapable of illustrating to you, the beautiful attributes and sublime virtues of Dr. Wadih Ameen.

[The following is the translation of the scan of the complete aforementioned handwritten letter which is included in the book.]

> Our dear son, Mr., Dr. Wadih Ameen,
>
> Greetings, peace and honor with the best wishes and the sincerest prayers that the Lord may support you, and make of you always a most impregnable fortress for humanity and a benefactor of the poor.
>
> Furthermore, I have received your letter, dated the 10th of the current month, and I have been trying to answer it by coming to you personally at the hospital to thank you for your exemplary humanity. Three times have I tried but with no success, because Mrs. Hosse is ill and her condition has caused me to change my appointments. Other affairs have also emerged which preoccupied me. I took the

first opportunity which I was offered by the coming of Mrs. Thoraia's husband who is ill in the hospital, so I hastened to compose this to you, that I may thank you greatly, for I love each person who sympathizes with the children of his nation, whenever the latter were poor or in need of care.

This lady earns her living from washing clothes in homes. Her husband is a poor man and they have five children who are in need of a lot, but what can they do? Therefore, I felt great happiness for what this unfortunate [woman] has received: your exceedingly great care and your merciful heart. For it is rare for people like her to be met whole-heartedly, and often they do not get a tenth of a tenth of your care, except rarely. The poor and needy do not get care except on the recommendation of a relative or the like. By God, however, I did not send her except for my knowledge of how bad her condition is. For she comes to wash the clothes but the illness sometimes prevents her from working [normally] except by spending twice the time. She comes two days in a row per week for one day's washing. Then she begged me to send her to the hospital though her children would have nobody to take care of them. So I sent her. I had prayed and asked the Lord Almighty to take care of her, so He prepared for her a man with a big heart like you. And if I thank you, it is out of my appreciation for each [government] worker doing his duty and a little more. For mercy is above justice.

I will strive, in the first opportunity, to visit your lordship, so that I may attain to seeing a man, [who is] noble, great, having precious morals. Until we meet, peace be to you, and the mercy of God. I congratulate you in advance, and all who are around you, for the blessed Feast of the Resurrection[30], and best wishes to you.

Sincerely,

[Signature]

P.S.: The husband (who is carrying this [letter]), Abdel Najar Mohammad Ali came, complaining that his children need the care of their ill mother. So I said to him, "What would you do if, God forbid, her illness hastens [her departure] and takes her?" I advised him to stay with the children or to send them to his neighbors in his absence, but he said that he had no neighbors!

By God, it is confounding. I hope that the Almighty grants her a speedy recovery, and that He grants us the same.

[Signature]

After that Dr. Wadih Ameen moved to El-Kalj Village near Cairo for work, where he was appointed a director of the hospital and the chief physician therein. Then in 1967, after the setback,[31] besides being the director of the hospital, he was appointed by the officials of the village its president as well,.

In 1969, he was transferred and promoted to the position of Health Inspector of Qalyub. At the same time, he opened for himself a private clinic in Qalyub Elbalad, and this was a source of great joy for many of the people of the town because they had a strong trust in him as a physician, as a skilled surgeon and as a faithful servant. Everyone in his town loved him,

---

30   Literally: Feast of the Passover.
31   1967 Arab-Israeli War.

Christians and Muslims [alike], after they noted that he did not discriminate between the rich and the poor, nor [between] a Christian and a Muslim. He would charge the examination fee only from the patients who could afford it, but as for the patient who could not afford it, he not only exempted them from paying for the examination, but he would give them the medication for free and ask for nothing in return. Here, we would like to relate a few nuggets of the noble acts which Dr. Wadih did for the patients he treated.

Artificial Limb

One day, a patient came to him, who had gangrene in his foot, and asked him to amputate the ailing foot. Dr. Wadih Ameen performed the amputation, and after the wound was healed following the operation, Dr. Wadih Ameen realized that the patient was unable to pay for an artificial limb which would help him move around. Therefore, Dr. Wadih bought for him an artificial limb at his personal expense and installed it for him so that the patient was able to move normally. This act brought joy into this patient's heart and he would always mention, at all times and to everyone, the favor that Dr. Wadih did for him.

No Need for Operation

One day, a patient came to Dr. Wadih in his private clinic, complaining of a pain in his kidneys. He showed him another doctor's opinion who had examined him first. That doctor's advice was that a surgical operation had to be performed on his kidneys, due to the lack of another medical alternative for treatment.

Dr. Wadih Ameen was silent for a moment, praying inaudibly a short prayer as he was accustomed to doing before beginning the examination on any patient. After the examination, he assured the patient that his condition did not call for a surgical operation. He brought him some pills, signed them with the sign of the cross, and gave them to the patient, praying for his healing once he finishes taking them.

After the patient finished taking the medication, he was completely healed, without doing any surgical operation. Many years passed on this incident and the pain did not return to the patient. However, years after, the patient suddenly felt that the same pain had returned, from which he had suffered years ago. He went to another physician for the examination, for by then Dr. Wadih had gone to the Monastery of the Syrians and had become a monk there. After the examination was done on the patient, the physician confessed that a surgical operation was necessary. The patient attempted to postpone the surgical operation to another time and to be content with the painkillers, [but] the physician utterly refused. Finally, the patient took out of his pocket an empty medication bottle, and he explained to the physician that years ago he suffered from the same pain and after taking this medication, he was completely healed and the pain did not return until this time.

The physician took the medication bottle and began inspecting it closely. He looked at the patient challengingly, saying, "It is impossible that this medication would heal you. You have to do the surgical operation. You must decide what you want to do." The patient left the doctor's clinic and decided within himself to take [the same] medication which he had taken years ago. On his way home, he turned to a pharmacy and bought the same medication which Dr. Wadih Ameen had given him years ago. After he went back home, he held the medication in his hand and signed it with the sign of the cross, and said, "May the blessing of Fr. Pimen be with me." By this faith, the patient began taking the medication and he was healed without performing any surgical operation. From that time on, the pain has not returned to him again.

His Patriotism

"Unless the LORD builds the house, they labor in vain who build it; unless the LORD guards the city, the watchman stays awake in vain."[32]

The patriotism of Dr. Wadih Ameen became known in all the regions where he had worked, and was confirmed by his faithfulness and honesty in his work and by showing no discrimination in his dealings with all. When officials in the country noted the patriotism of Dr. Wadih Ameen, they appointed him, after the setback in 1967, governor over El-Kalj Village, besides his work as a director of and physician in El-Kalj Hospital.

In this period, during the War of Attrition, some spies infiltrated El-Kalj Village. They came in as shoeblacks, but Dr. Wadih and those with him noticed that the clothes of these people did not match their work, as there were no signs of them using the paints used for shoes, nor were there signs of paint on their hands as is the case with shoeblacks who were widespread at that time. Also, the boxes they carried on their shoulders seemed new and clean, not having signs of previous use; amongst other things which made them suspicious about these men. After seizing them and interrogating them, they turned out to be spies working for the Israelite enemy. They sent them to the top authorities in the Egyptian military which, in turn, lauded the faithfulness, patriotism and vigilance of Dr.

---

32 Psalms 127:1.

Wadih Ameen.

The Success of the Service and Its Expansion

"But you shall receive power when the Holy Spirit has come upon you; and you shall be witnesses to Me."[33]

Dr. Wadih Ameen served in the service of Sunday School with all faithfulness, meekness and [self] sacrifice. He used to [not only] travel around preaching the Lord Jesus in all the villages and hamlets of the Qalyubia governorate, but also in every place he happened to be in. Therefore, the service in the city of Qalyub saw previously unmatched success and an expansion of the evangelical work outside the city of Qalyub. One of the fruits of the success of this service was the holding of the first annual conference for the districts of Qalyubia, the Sharkia, and the Monofia, and in attendance were delegates from some churches of Cairo and Giza, the theological seminary and the House of Sunday School of Rodd El-Farag. The idea of holding this conference came from the servants of Sunday School of Qalyub, first of whom was Dr. Wadih Ameen and the other servants from Qalyub Elbalad, in participation with Sunday School servants from Shaben El-Kanater. The conference was held in 1950 in the residence of the church of the great martyr St. George in Qalyub Elbalad, in the Diocese of His Eminence Bishop Youannis, metropolitan of Giza, Qalyubia, Kuesna Center, and East Atfeh. The classrooms of the Coptic Primary School, which adjoined the church building, were used for lodging more than seventy servants.

The proceedings of the conference began on the morning of Thursday July 27th, 1950 with the Divine

---

33 Acts 1:8.

Liturgy by the priest of the church, Hegumen Botros Gabriel, and the priest of St. George Church in Koum Ombo, Aswan, Hegumen Shenouda Kozzman. Important speeches in this conference were given by Mr. Nazir Gayed (H.H. Pope Shenouda III, may God prolong his life), representing the House of Sunday School in Rodd El-Farag, and the topic of his lecture was, "The Spiritual Life of the Servant;" and Dr. Waheeb Attalah (The late H.G. Bishop Gregorios), representing the theological seminary and the topic of his lecture was, "Orthodoxy and its Power in the Service." Also in attendance was Dr. Meleka Eskander from Shaben El-Kanater (Hangmen Mina Eskander of Alexandria) and many [other] prominent servants.

So remained Dr. Wadih Ameen faithful in his service in Sunday School classes in the city of Qalyub Elbalad, and the villages and hamlets of Qalyubia governorate for thirty years, which began in 1942 until 1972 when he left the world and went to the monastery of the Virgin Lady, [known as] of the Syrians.

His Calling for the Priesthood

"Therefore, brethren, be even more diligent to make your call and election sure, for if you do these things you will never stumble."[34]

The service of Dr. Wadih Ameen was not limited to the range of his town only, but it extended and expanded until it encompassed many governorates of Egypt. Through these regions, from Alexandria to Aswan, he would wander preaching and teaching the people the way of salvation, after his fame for being faithful in service and the purity of his orthodox teachings spread far and wide.

---

34 2 Peter 1:10.

One day, he received an invitation from H.E. Abba Makarius, metropolitan of Qena and its surroundings, to give a sermon in a weeklong revival organized by the Diocese of Qena. The following is an excerpt of the invitation sent by the Diocese of Qena to Dr. Wadih:

Qena, 15/12/1966

My beloved brother, Dr. Wadih,

I send you my greetings and my heartfelt affections, wishing for you and your family all health and peace from our Lord Jesus Christ, who is able to help you and strengthen you in all your services.

We were all pleased by your acceptance of our invitation regarding holding a spiritual revival in Qena. You will find us longing, to the utmost, to see you and to hear the words of grace which the Lord will grant you. Of course, there is no specific program, but the matter is left to you and to what God guides you to. We would like to let you know that the topics which H.G. Abba Shenouda (Bishop of Education, and currently H.H. Pope Shenouda) delved into in his sermons, were on fasting, communion, the tongue, studying the Holy Bible, intercession, prayer. The Lord is able to help you choose suitable topics.

When Dr. Wadih Ameen arrived at Qena, he met H.E. Abba Makarius to take his blessing. His Eminence revealed to him his desire of ordaining him priest in the Diocese, but Dr. Wadih was surprised by the words which he did not anticipate. He felt that he did not know at all how to answer the metropolitan, but with profuse politeness, he apologized to him [for declining the offer], for he had had it in his heart to leave the world and to go to the monastery. But before he left, [H.E.] Abba Makarius asked him to pray that God's will and desire may be revealed.

On the next morning, before Dr. Wadih left the residence of the metropolitan, he again met H.E. Abba Makarius, who began by asking, "Did you see something at night? Did something appear to you?" Dr. Wadih answered saying, "I didn't see anything." Here, Abba Makarius spoke what was in Dr. Wadih's heart and said, "You want to be a monk, my son?" Dr. Wadih said to him, "I wish, Your Eminence; I really do." So Abba Makarius blessed him and left him to his desire, and he did not open the topic of the priesthood with him again.

Frequenting the Monastery of the Syrians

> "How lovely is Your tabernacle, O LORD of hosts!
> My soul longs, yes, even faints for the courts of
> the LORD; my heart and my flesh cry out for the
> living God."[35]

We had previously mentioned that, after reading the stories of the monks in the book "Taming the Minds in the Paradise of the Monks" by the monk Hegumen Armanius Habashi El-Baramawy, Dr. Wadih Ameen's heart cleaved to the monastic life and loved it since he was thirteen years old.

His love and longing for this life increased after he met Fr. Mina the Solitary (the late H.H. Pope Kyrillos VI) in 1948, when he was nineteen years old. The young Wadih could not bridle his love and longing for the monastic life, and expressed what was in his heart to Fr. Mina the Solitary, that perhaps he may find rest and

---
35 Psalms 84:1–2.

a solution with him. From his exceedingly great love for the monastic life, he longed to leave medical school when he was still in his first year that he may go to the monastery. But in wisdom and moderation, Fr. Mina the Solitary calmed him down and advised him to tarry and not to go to the monastery until he has finished his studies and received his degree in medicine. He directed him also not to leave his mother alone, and that it was his duty not to go to the monastery except after she had passed away. At the end of the conversation, Dr. Wadih Ameen obeyed the words of his guide and his teacher, Fr. Mina the Solitary.

After graduating from medical school, Dr. Wadih Ameen began frequenting the monastery of the Lady Virgin, of the Syrians, in 1955. There, he met many of the fathers the monks and the monastery's great elders such as Fr. Youssef the Great, Fr. Samuel Tawadros, and Fr. Philips the Great who passed away at the age of about 105 years. During his visit to the monastery, he met his colleagues with whom he had served, such as Fr. Antonios of the Syrians (H.H. Pope Shenouda III, may God grant him health) and Fr. Shenouda of the Syrians (the late [H.G.] Abba Youannis, Bishop of Garbia).

In one of his frequent retreats in the monastery of the Syrians, he met in the retreat house the young man Samir Kheer Sukar (H.E. Abba Pachomius, metropolitan of the Beheira and the Five Western Cities), where they had the opportunity to form a strong friendship with each other.

In [another] one of Dr. Wadih Ameen's frequent retreats in the monastery of the Syrians, he happened to be in the monastery on the day Br. Ameen Nasr (H.E. Abba Arsenius, metropolitan of Minia and Abu Karkas) was ordained a monk.

Due to his frequent visits to the monastery of the Syrians, a strong trust was formed between Dr. Wadih and the Abba Theophilus, the abbot of the monastery, that he gave him the keys to one of the cells to always keep with him, so that whenever he came to retreat, he may stay in it.

In one of the retreats he spent in the monastery of the Syrians in 1968, Dr. Wadih met Hegumen Hanna Ibrahim, one of the elders of the monastery of the Syrians. He had the gift of copying manuscripts with inexpressible exactness. He agreed with Dr. Wadih to buy paper, ink and whatever else he needed for copying, so that he may copy for him the book of "The Great Among the Knowledgeable, Mar Isaac the Syrian." Indeed, he did copy the manuscript and gave it to Dr. Wadih. I would like to point out here that this copy of the manuscript is the one Fr. Samuel of the Syrians (the late Abba Samuel, Bishop of Sheben El-kanater) photocopied and made a special printing of it for the monks of the monasteries. He did not, [however,] omit from the manuscript the last paragraph where the name of Dr. Wadih Ameen was inserted.

Every time he came to the monastery of the Syrians for retreat, Dr. Wadih Ameen was in the habit of going up to the Church of Archangel Michael inside the fort of the monastery, that he may pray there his psalms and his personal prayers. It happened one time that as he was standing for prayer in the church inside the fort, his heart aflame in prayer, being very joyful and comforted, that he felt something unusual around him. His heart began to be troubled, and his body trembled and shivered. When he looked back, he saw the enemy of good in the form of a black figure, and a very foul stench emanated from him. He quickly turned his gaze away, beseeching God in a loud voice to protect him from the plots of Satan. He then completed his prayer with all trust in the mercy of our Lord Jesus Christ, spending a long time in profound prayer which made him forget who was behind him, and with God's grace the enemy of good departed in great shame.

After finishing his prayer in the Church of Archangel Michael in the fort, Dr. Wadih Ameen went down the stairs, and as usual when Fr. Faltaous of the Syrians, who was living in a cell inside the monastery's fort, heard footsteps on the stairs, he called with a loud voice from inside his cell, "Who is going down the stairs?" Dr. Wadih answered and made himself known. Then Fr. Faltaous opened the door of his cell and brought him in, saying, "Come in, my brother, come in." He prepared a cup of tea, then talked with him about the lives of the saints and the anchorite fathers and about other spiritual matters for many hours.

Of these meetings and spiritual conversations between Fr. Faltaous and Dr. Wadih Ameen, Fr. Pimen says, "I remember in one of the sittings with Fr. Faltaous, that I sat with him after Vespers and I asked him about humility. He continued talking to me about humility throughout the night, nonstop, until the bell for Midnight [Praises] rang, and the bell for Morning Raising of Incense rang, and finally he said to me, 'This is enough, my brother. With this we have finished the introduction on humility.' Then he prayed for me and blessed me, and I left him to attend the Divine Liturgy."

Successive Signs and Clear Callings

"I will instruct you and teach you in the way you should go; I will guide you with My eye."[36]

---

36 Psalms 32:8.

Departing from the world to the wilderness is not an easy thing, requiring from a person great struggle and divine help to support him. In likewise manner, one of the fathers in the Paradise of the Fathers expressed this idea, saying, "Marvel not at a man who leaves the wilderness and goes to the world, but all the more marvel at a man who has left the world and gone to the wilderness."[37] For the man who leaves the raging sea of the world, going to the calm wilderness is likened to a man swimming against the current in a raging sea, but he who leaves the wilderness for the world is like a man walking on foot to get into the raging sea of the world which is full of dangers.

Leaving the world, therefore, requires from a person a violent struggle and divine grace so that he may be liberated from its many bonds and may ascend to the highest glories. The more numerous and the stronger the bonds of the world are, the greater the struggle is and the greater the need for divine help to support him.

Such was Dr. Wadih Ameen's situation, for many bonds had wrapped around him, trying to hinder him from fulfilling his wish. His strong determination however, and the clarity of the goal before him, were stronger than these bonds. One of these bonds was his social status as a successful physician and skilled surgeon, occupying the position of Health Inspector of Qalyub and owning a private clinic that was sought after by many patients. This is besides the responsibility laid upon him of taking care of his elderly mother. Besides these bonds and others, there was the bond of service, which included the responsibility of preaching and teaching, the stewardship of the service, and other responsibilities which were laid upon him. One might

---

37   Cf. *The Paradise of the Holy Fathers* 2, Budge A.W., trans. (London, UK: Chatto & Windus, 1907), 253.

not consider the responsibilities of service as bonds preventing a person from leaving the world to go to the monastery, but it is, undoubtedly, one of the obstacles and strong bonds that have tied many, making them incapable of being liberated and going to the monastery.

When divine grace saw Dr. Wadih Ameen's sincere intention and faithful struggle, it supported him with great power, thereby enabling him to be liberated from all the bonds of the world, so that he may take off for the wilderness.

Here, we shall stand together, dear reader, to observe the work of divine grace in overcoming the obstacles which obstructed Dr. Wadih's departure from the world, and also in giving him a powerful push until he could take off for the monastery of the Syrians.

The Appearance of the Lady the Virgin

Dr. Wadih Ameen's niece was sick with a high fever, so he went to his sister's house to treat her. After she began to feel better, Dr. Wadih noticed that his brother-in-law was suffering from neck pain, and upon examination, he was found to have a large abscess in his neck. Dr. Wadih decided to perform a simple operation, to open and sterilize it. After completing this successfully, the time was very late; therefore, he stayed overnight at his sister and her husband's place.

In the morning, Dr. Wadih woke up from sleep, left his room, and sat with his sister and her husband. During their conversation, Dr. Wadih said to his sister, "Your apartment is blessed." His sister inquired about the reason that made him say this, and after [she] greatly persisted, he found no way out but to reveal the reason. He said to her, "Our Lady the Virgin appeared to me in the room where I was sleeping." While his sister and her husband were glad about this appearance with which their house was blessed, Dr. Wadih Ameen, however, had the greater joy and greater consolation by this appearance, for he considered it a calling from the Lady the Virgin for him to go to her monastery: The monastery of the Lady the Virgin Mary, of the Syrians.

An Answered Prayer

In those days, the thought of leaving the world and going to the monastery was the all-absorbing occupation which dominated Dr. Wadih's mind. Because of this thought, nights would pass sleepless but for fleeting minutes.

On one of the days, Dr. Wadih left his room after midnight and sat in a chair on the balcony, and his soul was sorrowful from the many obstacles which prevented him from going to the monastery, such as his work, his service, the care for his mother about whom Pope Kyrillos VI had given him command. Pope Kyrillos had passed away in those days, thereby intensifying his sorrows.

After long hours deep in thought, time approached three in the morning. He rose up from his chair that very hour, his heart having incited him to prayer, and stood praying with tears, lifting up his heart to God, that He may make ready for him a way out of the world, and may eliminate the obstacles, especially the responsibility of his work as Health Inspector of Qalyub and the Hospital of Qalyub management. After finishing his prayer, behold, he heard a voice from heaven like thunder, though it was summer at the time. Then, profound peace came into his heart with a sure feeling that his prayers were lifted up to heaven, and that his supplications had entered the Divine Presence.

Overcoming the Obstacles

Three days after Dr. Wadih's prayer, the hindrances began to dissolve and the obstacles to be resolved, one by one. A new physician came and was assigned to work in Qalyub Elbalad Hospital, who was entrusted with one of the units. He was followed by another physician who came a week after. An assistant physician came to the Internal Medicine Department, and this physician took over Dr. Wadih's position; this was Bishop Moussa's brother, the bishop of Youth.

This is how the hand of God was overcoming the hindrances one by one; however, one hindrance remained, blocking his way. This was the word Pope Kyrillos gave him: "Do not go to the monastery except after the death of your mother." How God removed this hindrance is what we will see next.

The Appearance of Two Elders Beside Him

In one of the nights, Dr. Wadih went to his room, as his custom was, and sat on the couch, continuing his prayers and meditations. That night, he saw two elders, who were monks, sitting one on his right-hand and the other on his left. When he saw them, he extended both of his arms and embraced the elders and asked them to take him with them. He said to them, "Take me with you. It is enough. I have no desire in the world." The elders then answered him, saying, "Fear not, you will come soon." They, then, disappeared. Afterwards, he experienced great joy, being convinced that these two elders were Abba Anthony, the father of monks, and Abba Macarius the Great, coming to confirm his calling for monasticism, and that the time for his departure to the monastery was approaching. This occurred a few days before going to the monastery.

An Appearance and Incense for Blessing

All the obstacles were overcome and none remained but one only. This took the foremost importance in all of Dr. Wadih's prayers, and every day, he waited for a spiritual sign by which he may know that Pope Kyrillos was pleased and had approved of him leaving to the monastery. He continually asked for his intercessions on this matter.

Heaven did not delay in answering Dr. Wadih's prayers, but declared its approval to him. It happened that while Dr. Wadih was driving his car, Pope Kyrillos VI appeared to him on the side of the road. Pope Kyrillos threw with his hand a handful of incense into the car, and disappeared immediately after. Dr. Wadih noticed what had happened, stopped his car on the side of the road and got out of it, and began collecting the grains of incense scattered inside his Mercedes car. He placed the incense in a glass jar which he kept in his cell, even until the time of his passing. After this occurrence took place, Dr. Wadih's heart became at ease and he considered it a sign of the approval of Pope Kyrillos VI of him to go to the monastery.

The Last Blessing Before His Departure

After the revelation of Pope Kyrillos' approval and his blessing, Dr. Wadih took his final decision to depart to the monastery. He began emptying his private clinic, leaving it for one of his colleagues. When the content of the clinic was being collected, to vacate it, the nurse came in to tell him about a poor man in worn-out clothes who was standing outside by the clinic's door. This man did not want to speak to her at all, and he refused to take from her any alms. She did not know what he wanted.

Dr. Wadih came out of his room and headed toward the door to see who was this marvelous poor man, of whom the nurse spoke. He saw a skinny man wearing a white loose garment and a white cap on his head, who seemed to be no more than one of the very destitute. Dr. Wadih asked him, "Do you need something? Are you sick?" But he did not answer him at all.

Therefore, when Dr. Wadih saw this, he took from his pocket some money and offered it to him. The man gave him a piercing look, smiled and took nothing from his hand. Finally, he turned around and left. Moments later, Dr. Wadih realized that this was the late Fr. Abdel Messih of Manahra. He went after him quickly that he may find him, and began calling him, but he could find no trace of him. He was very sorrowful about this but knew that he came to bless him and bless the decision of his departure to the monastery.

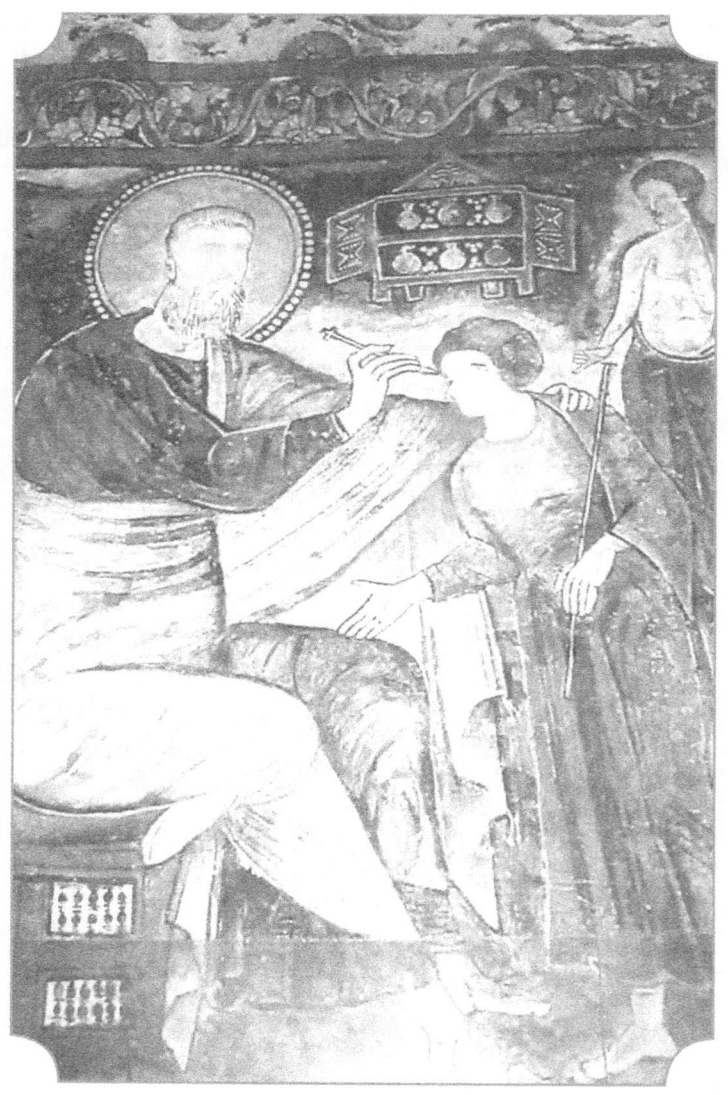

PART ONE

Father Pimen's Life

CHAPTER TWO

His Monastic Life

The Journey to the Monastery

> "You hold me by my right hand. You will guide me with Your counsel, and afterward receive me to glory. Whom have I in heaven but You? And there is none upon earth that I desire besides You."[38]

> "So I said, 'Oh, that I had wings like a dove! I would fly away and be at rest. Indeed, I would wander far off, and remain in the wilderness.'"[39]

After Dr. Wadih had decided to leave the world and go to the monastery, he began taking practical steps in utter secrecy, being cautious about news leaking to his family, in fear that they may hinder and prevent him from going to the monastery.

The first step was to change the color of his Mercedes from sky blue to black so that the car color may be in agreement with the new monastic life he was to pursue in the monastery. Afterwards, he began taking his books and personal belongings gradually every day, storing them in his private room in the hospital. Meanwhile, he sold his private clinic and submitted his resignation from work. Finally, he handed over the responsibility of the stewardship of Sunday School service, and with this, he ended all his bonds with the world in preparation for the journey to the monastery of the Syrians.

Here, we leave the conversation to Fr. Pimen to narrate the events of that night, in which he travelled from his town till his arrival at the monastery of the Syrians. His reverence says:

> When the fullness of time had come which God chose for me to go to the monastery of the Syrians, it was on the eve of the 23rd of October,

---
38 Psalms 73:23–25.
39 Psalms 55:6–7.

1972. I had put all the clinic's essentials and a complete operation room in a transport truck. When the time was approaching three in the morning, I left my house, got into my car, drove to the place where I had hidden my personal belongings, and put them in the car. Then, I began the journey to the monastery.

After I drove a long distance, I began driving in the desert road. Drowsiness was overcoming me, so I thought that I'd better park the car on the side of the road and take a little nap before proceeding on the journey. But I said to myself, "The road is isolated and the time is late. I might be attacked by a bandit." Then I lifted up my heart and prayed to my God, and said to Him, "Lord, You help me and protect me, and You are the one taking me to the monastery in peace. And Your will and Your good desire be done." And after I completed my prayer, drowsiness overcame me and I could not resist it. During this time, I did not feel anything at all, and the car was moving on its way on its own, without me controlling it at all. After a while—I do not know how much time had passed while I was unconscious—I was roused from my sleep to find myself near the Rest House. Minutes later, I found myself steps away from the monastery of the Syrians.

Joining the Monastery and His Ordination a Monk

"Blessed are those who were drunk with Your love, O my God, because by their inebriation in You, they forgot their old life."
—The Spiritual Elder—

After a distressful journey, full of dangers, Dr. Wadih Ameen arrived at the monastery of the Lady Virgin Mary, renowned as [the monastery] of the Syrians, in the morning of the 24th of October, 1972. The monks received him with love and joy, for he was known to the monks of the monastery of the Syrians, on account of his frequent visits to the monastery since 1955. Some of the monks took him to H.G. Abba Theophilus the abbot of the monastery, who received him with joy, love and great esteem. The following day, the transport truck arrived at the monastery. Abba Theophilus gave him two cells on the fourth floor of the building of the cells, that he may put in them the tools of his clinic and of the operation room, which he brought with him to the monastery, thereby becoming the first clinic and first operation room in Coptic monasteries.

We leave the conversation to Fr. Pimen to tell us of his first memories with Abba Theophilus and how his ordination a monk took place. His reverence says:

> Abba Theophilus took me to his cell and handed me one of his cassocks, and said to me, "Try it on and see if it fits you." And when I put it on, I found that it fit me very well. So he said to me, "Keep it on, and also don't shave your beard [any longer]." Then he gave me a cell to live in.
>
> A few days after my arrival at the monastery

of the Syrians, my mother and my siblings came to the monastery for their first visit to see me. When they met me, they tried in various ways to persuade me to go back with them, but they did not succeed before my firm resoluteness. They, then, met Abba Theophilus, the abbot of the monastery, and brought their complaint of me to him, seeking that perhaps he could persuade me to go back with them. He answered them in wisdom and shrewdness, saying, "This [man] has had the key to his cell with him for a long time, [even] before coming to the monastery." He, then, sat with them and spoke to them about the vanities of the passing world, and of the glory their son will gain in choosing this path. After he calmed and consoled them by such words, he dismissed them in peace, and they left on their way back to their town.

But the matter was neither easy nor simple for his mother to accept, especially in the beginning, for she was left alone in the house. Divine care, however, did not leave her, but God sent her consolation from time to time. On one night, after she went to her room, being troubled and thinking about her loneliness, she heard a strange voice coming from outside [her room]. She was initially afraid but was surprised to see a young man whose face was white and shining, wearing a general's outfit, standing in front of her in the room. He said to her, "Do not be afraid. You are under my protection and not alone. If you need anything, call me." She asked him, "Who are you? Do I know you? Where do you come from? And where will you be, so that I may call you?" He answered, "I am with you in the living room outside." He, then, disappeared. She quickly went out to the living room and turned on the lights. Her eyes instantly fell on a large icon hung in the living room of the great martyr St. George. She immediately identified the features of the general who appeared to her and spoke with her seconds ago; it was St. George, the Martyr.

Fr. Pimen continues his conversation, saying:

> About ten days after coming to the monastery, we heard the bells of Abba Pishoy monastery, ringing to announce the arrival of His Holiness Pope Shenouda III to his residence in Abba Pishoy monastery. He was returning from a trip to Russia. Abba Theophilus went to greet him and he took me with him. After we greeted H.H. Pope [Shenouda], Abba Theophilus asked him saying, "Do you know this brother?" The Pope thought that I was a new priest, spending my forty-day period at the monastery after the ordination, to receive the Divine Liturgy. This is because my look inspired this: a short beard, wearing a cap and black cassock. His Holiness said, "Is he a priest receiving the Liturgy?" Abba Theophilus answered him saying, "This is Dr. Wadih Ameen, coming for monasticism." Pope Shenouda looked at me and recognized me, for he had known me for a long time since the time when we served together in Sunday School before His Holiness went to the monastery of the Syrians. His Holiness congratulated me for joining the monastery and prayed for me that I may be blessed and confirmed. H.G. Abba Theophilus, then, approached H.H. the Pope and they spoke together about ordaining me a monk the next day. Finally, we greeted His Holiness and left in peace heading back to the monastery of the Syrians.

When we arrived at the monastery of the Syrians, Abba Theophilus ordered that they ring the Vespers' bell, to pray the Vespers Raising of Incense. After praying the Psalms, he gave me the monastic form with the name the monk Pimen. I spent that whole night in the Church, keeping vigil, as the custom is, and listened to the words and advice of my fathers the monks, throughout the night. After finishing the Midnight Praises and Morning Raising of Incense, His Holiness Pope Shenouda III came to the monastery of the Syrians. H.H. Pope Shenouda, along with Abba Theophilus, the abbot, ordained me a monk with the name Pimen. It was on Sunday, the 5th of November, 1972, which is the 26th of Paone 1689 AM. I attended Liturgy and proceeded to take Communion. The monks paraded me in a procession inside the Church, while singing beautiful hymns, and it was a great joy for the monastery and the monks. Finally, I went back to my cell and began looking forward to starting my new life.

Spiritual Activity and Medical Services

"Fervent in spirit, serving the Lord."[40]

Fr. Pimen started his monastic life with fiery spiritual longings and great spiritual activity, like a thirsty land for water[41] and like a deer for the water brooks[42]. His commitment and seriousness were manifest in the orderliness with which he attended Praises, Liturgy, and Vesper prayers. This is besides his seriousness in

---

40 Romans 12:11.
41 Ezekiel 19:13; Psalms 63:1.
42 Psalms 42:1.

his personal prayers, prostrations and fasts within his cell. Because the fathers the monks knew of his copious knowledge, especially that of the Holy Scriptures, their gatherings with him were characterized by conversations and discussions on Holy Scriptures and on some verses that were difficult to understand.

Besides his spiritual activity, he offered medical services to all who were sick from the monks and from the workers in the monastery. His medical services were also extended to include those sick in Abba Pishoy and Baramos monasteries, which he offered, not only to the monks, but also to the workers in the monastery and all visitors of the monastery who needed urgent treatment. After examining a patient, whoever they may be, he used to give away the appropriate medication, with no cost, from the medications he had brought with him or from the medications that were donated to the monastery.

The monks of the monastery of the Syrians, the other monasteries, and also the workers, felt the love and [value of] service Fr. Pimen offered them, which he did, not with reluctance or grumbling, but with joy and utmost love. This was manifest whenever he went by his car to the Baramos or Abba Pishoy monasteries to treat a patient, whoever they may be, whether a monk or worker. Often, out of necessity, he used to return to the monastery of the Syrians to bring an injection or a medication which he did not have in his car [with him] and go back to the monasteries again. Also, the patient's treatment in these monasteries, often needed a change to be made for the wound every day for several days. Undoubtedly, as a skilled physician of the sicknesses of the body and spirit, he used to rejoice and strive to give comfort to every patient groaning from the cruelty of illness.

Overseeing The Retreat House

> "For even the Son of Man did not come to be served, but to serve, and to give His life a ransom for many."[43]

H.G. Abba Theophilus, the abbot of the monastery, seeing that Fr. Pimen had a great power of love, ardor, [a spirit of] giving, and copious knowledge, endeavored to make good use of [these qualities]. Therefore, His Grace entrusted him with overseeing the retreat house. He oversaw the cleanliness of the house and the cleanliness of the residence rooms, and also oversaw the cooking and the preparation of the food for the young men. He used to organize for them a schedule for attending Praise services, Liturgy and retreating in the mountain. He also sat with them after Vesper prayers every day to give them a spiritual talk and to listen to their questions, which used to pour down on him nonstop for long hours. He would answer them with patience, long-suffering and simplicity, with an ability to persuade every inquirer. Therefore, many of these young men were drawn to the life of repentance, and others to the monastic path, because of his abundant knowledge and open-mindedness, along with his lofty spirituality.

---

43 Mark 10:45.

Overseeing the retreat house in these days was not an easy endeavor, owing to the fact that great numbers of young men were flocking to it. The retreat house of the monastery of the Syrians was the first among all Coptic monasteries. It was a shining beacon that enlightened the minds of young men, and a warm fort embracing them from the world's vain temptations. Many of the young men on retreat asked him for private appointments to sit with him individually for confession and spiritual guidance, or to ask his opinion on some of life's affairs. I will let you imagine, dear reader, that all this dire exertion and exhausting labor which had fallen on the shoulders of Fr. Pimen were beside his monastic canon which he did in his private cell.

In truth, until recently, near the time of his departure, and after he had handed over the responsibility of the retreat house to another monk, he gave a weekly sermon to the young men in the retreat house and had private sittings with whoever asked him for confession or guidance.

The Continual Flight and the Standing Snare

> "Therefore when Jesus perceived that they were about to come and take Him by force to make Him king, He departed again to the mountain by Himself alone."[44]

Fr. Pimen ardently loved the monastic life with all his heart, and yearned to spend all his life within the fold of the monastery of the Syrians. Therefore, he ran away repeatedly from H.G. Abba Theophilus the abbot, who tried many times to ordain him priest. Fr. Pimen did not desire to be ordained priest. Because of his past strong acquaintance with H.H. the Pope before monasticism,

---

44 John 6:15.

and because of his excellent effective service, these incited him to run away lest his ordination a priest becomes an encouraging incentive to be asked to go out for service, thereby leaving the monastery which he loved with all his heart.

Although Fr. Pimen succeeded in escaping many times from Abba Theophilus, and his ordination did not take place, he could not escape this very time. He was ordained a priest by a clever ploy contrived by Abba Theophilus, the abbot. Here I leave you, dear reader, with Fr. Pimen to tell you about the plan contrived to ordain him priest. His reverence says:

> I remained five years running away from every attempt done by Abba Theophilus to ordain me a priest. This was in fear of making me leave against my will for service.
>
> Owing to my previous acquaintance with H.H. Pope Shenouda III, His Holiness sent me an invitation to serve in America, and another time to serve in Kenya, but I could not accept [either] out of my superabundant ardent love for the monastic life inside the monastery of the Syrians. Therefore, I politely apologized, explaining to him the reason for the refusal. For this [reason] also, I ran away repeatedly from being ordained a priest, lest this becomes a reason for my going down for service and leaving the monastery.
>
> Therefore, my ordination a priest was done by a trick planned by Abba Theophilus, the abbot, especially after I repeatedly escaped for five years. One of the consequences of my delayed ordination a priest was that the monks who were ordained monks after me moved ahead

of me in [the monastic] order[45] after they were ordained priests. Here is how the thought-out plan went on:

The bell [of the monastery] rang, and Abba Theophilus and the monks gathered in the *Doxar*[46] of the Church of the Cave for Vespers. Things were going on very normally. After the prayer ended, each monk came forward according to their monastic order to do a prostration to the abbot and kiss his hand, and so [each monk] proceeded to greet his brothers the monks who stood in line after they had greeted the abbot and the monks standing after him. When my turn came, I stepped forward and made a prostration to H.G. Abba Theophilus, then stood up as usual to kiss his hand. I was surprised, however, that he took a hold of my head forcefully with his hand. He, then, pointed to some of the monks to prevent me from leaving, in case I attempted to run away from him. Standing to the right side of the bishop was Fr. Youssef the great who also held my hand firmly so that I would not escape. I tried to wriggle from under the hand of the bishop and the hand of Fr. Youssef to escape, but I could not this time. In the end, I gave in to the will of God and stood still. His Grace placed his hand on me and pronounced the three signings. So I was made a priest from that moment. He said to me, "Tomorrow you have to attend the Liturgy so that we may complete the rite of the ordination." The next morning, I attended Liturgy and did not run away as before,

---

45   Or: rank.

46   The *Doxar*: a Syriac word which means the outer entrance of the Church. The monks of the monastery of the Syrians are accustomed to praying Vespers in the *Doxar* of the Church of the Cave during the Winter [season]. (Author's note).

because I felt that my running away this time would be a kind of obstinacy, pride, insistence on [my] opinion, and disobedience which are conducts that disagree with the monastic [way of] life. My ordination to the priesthood was on Monday, 28th of March, 1978, which is the 18th of Paremhotep, 1694 AM. Two years and few months later, H.G. Abba Theophilus promoted me to the hegumeny, on Sunday, 24th of August, 1980, which is the 18th Mesore, 1696 AM. He ordained, on the same day, Hegumen Archilidis of the Syrians, Hegumen Barsanuphius of the Syrians, and Hegumen Moussa of the Syrians (H.G. Abba Athanasious, Bishop of Beni Mazar).

"Honor flees away from before the man that runs after it; but he who flees from it, the same will it hunt down, and will become to all men a herald of his humility."[47]

—St. Isaac the Syrian—

---

47   *The Ascetical Homilies of Saint Isaac the Syrian.* (Boston, MA: Holy Transfiguration Monastery, 2011), 166.

A Lover of the Wilderness on Moonlit Nights

"Go out with Him into the wilderness and ascend with Him the mountains and sit quietly down at His feet with the beasts which came to be comforted by their Lord. And there, arise with Him to learn warfare and fighting with the enemies."

—The Spiritual Elder—

Moonlit nights in the wilderness are nights enchanting. The fathers who had tasted their beauty described them by a saying, very simple and deep at the same time. They said, "Sleep in these nights is accursed!" From their superabundant love for nighttime, they devoted it for prayer. Therefore, St. Isaac says, "The night is separated for the labor of prayer." How magnificent and beautiful it is for the human soul to walk with her heavenly Bridegroom in the stillness of the night, with the gentleness of the air and the dim light of the moon, bestowing humbleness and the fear of God within the soul. It lifts her up to the bridal chamber[48] of the heavenly Bridegroom. There, the soul is poured and dissolves before her heavenly Bridegroom, in prayer and spiritual soliloquy, thereby the divine treasures are opened to her and she takes abundantly until she says to Him, "Enough, enough."

It is difficult for those living in cities to taste this beauty amid the noise, the hustle and the bustle coming out of every place, besides the intense lights emanating from shops, cars and advertisements. They are, by all these, deprived of these divine gifts and heavenly blessings.

---

48 See Psalms 18:5 LXX; Rite of Monk Ordination, Funeral Exposition.

Fr. Pimen was tightly attached to the wilderness and his attachment was especially intensified on moonlit nights, to the point of ardent love. Therefore, he made sure to take walks in the mountain in these nights, whether alone or with a group of monks. He would spend his night singing psalms, and at times meditating or conversing with his God in deep prayer of the heart, in love and boldness; and at other times he would keep silent in the stillness of the night, to listen to God's voice for him. When the night approaches its end, he would take part with the irrational creation in praising God; with the birds and animals, the sun and air, and the mountains, and Fr. Pimen [with them], all forming a beautiful chorus, singing to God a song of thanksgiving, honor and glorification. With the dawning of the day, he would bring his sojourn to an end, returning back to the monastery.

Here I leave you, dear reader, with Fr. Pimen to relate to you the things that happened to him in one of these nights. His reverence says:

> We were accustomed to go, in the full-moon nights (13th, 14th and 15th days of the lunar month) to the empty sea region, which was located about seven or eight kilometers from the monastery. We would spend the whole night in prayer, praise and meditation, in the moonlight.
>
> In these days, we were a group consisting of five or six monks who went together to the mountain. Each one in the group brought something with him. One brought bread, another water, a third brought a psalmody book, and so on. We walked separately at a distance from each other so that we may spend some solitary time. Afterwards, we would gather and

sit together to rest and meditate, then pray Midnight Praises together in the moonlight, and at the approaching of the dawn, we would return to the monastery.

When the enemy of good saw our constancy at keeping this retreat over a long time, he envied us and desired to terrify our hearts and scare us, that we may not return to the mountain again. One night, it happened after we had walked a long distance from the monastery, that he appeared to us in the form of a huge dragon which had wings, and he began revolving over us while giving off very troubling sounds like the hissing of snakes. I alone saw him but the rest of the monks heard the noise. This introduced fear and disturbance into our hearts, so that some of the fathers suggested that it would be better to go back to the monastery, in fear that something bad befalls us. But I said to them, "Do not be afraid; stay calm." We then sat down on the sand for a while until our disturbance dissipated. We, then, stood for prayer and praises, and after we spent our night in the mountain, we returned to the monastery again. We were all certain that what had happened was a war from the enemy of good to disturb us and scare us, so that we may stop going out to the mountain again, and thereby lose the enjoyment of the blessings of these nights which gave us joy and consolation.

Healing His Ailing Hand

> "He said to the man, 'Stretch out your hand.' And he stretched it out, and his hand was restored as whole as the other."[49]

Fr. Pimen suffered from an injury to his left hand which made him incapable of moving it at all. A few days after the injury, he met Fr. Faltaous and told him about his hand which caused him pain and which he could not move. He asked him to pray that it may be healed, but Fr. Faltaous refrained and quickly ran away. Fr. Pimen followed him and admonished him saying, "You pray and heal people [coming from] outside, and we, your children, you leave us like this." Fr. Faltaous answered him [saying,] "No my brother, I'm not the kind doing such things[50], my brother." Fr. Pimen said to him, "I will tell Pope Kyrillos about you." He left him and went back to his cell.

Returning to his cell, Fr. Pimen stood praying, and in his prayer, he complained about Fr. Faltaous to Pope Kyrillos. A few hours later, Fr. Faltaous came to Fr. Pimen and knocked on his cell's door. When he opened to him, Fr. Faltaous said, smiling, "So you've complained about me to Pope Kyrillos!" Then he took out a bottle of oil, and said to Fr. Pimen, "Come look my brother; see who is going to sign the oil."

When Fr. Faltaous began signing the oil, a luminous hand appeared and signed the oil. Immediately the oil began bubbling up inside the bottle until it almost

---

49 Mark 3:5.
50 That is, doing miracles.

overflowed. Fr. Faltaous asked Fr. Pimen, saying, "You know whose hand this is, my brother?" Fr. Pimen answered him, "Of course I know; he was my father of confession. This is Pope Kyrillos' hand." Fr. Faltaous, then, anointed him with the oil and went away. A few hours later, Fr. Pimen felt that his hand was completely healed and he could move it as he wished, through the blessing of Pope Kyrillos VI and Fr. Faltaous of the Syrians.

Seeing A Spiritual Procession

"So it was that the beggar died, and was carried by the angels to Abraham's bosom."[51]

One of the monastic practices which Fr. Pimen loved was spending the night watchful in ceaseless prayer and meditation. It happened on the 8th of the month of Kiahk, AD 1976, that he went out of his cell at night. His cell was on the third floor of the building of the cells in the ancient [part of the] monastery. He sat down outside for prayer and meditation. In these days, the air in the monastery was bathed in spirituality; calmness and stillness reigned over the monastery, dim candle lights illuminated the cells, and gas lamps illuminated the pathways in the monastery.

When the time approached three in the morning, Fr. Pimen saw a wondrous scene. A large disc of light

---

51 Luke 16:22.

appeared in front of him above Abba Pishoy monastery and was moving towards the monastery of the Syrians. The closer it came, the clearer and larger it appeared. Therefore, he was drawn to this spiritual scene and stared intently at it. In the forefront of the procession was a man, and behind him was a great number of angels spanning a distance of about 500 meters. They were praising in the air and the man who was leading the procession appeared to be kneeling, slightly leaning forward, greatly analogous [in posture] to the icon of St. Stephen the Martyr when was kneeling at the time of his stoning. They sang a melodious hymn, its tune akin to that of "In the Name" hymn. The procession moved closer towards Fr. Pimen until it appeared very clearly before him, which then moved beside his cell between the building of the cells in the ancient monastery and the lighthouse, thereby going out of his sight. Fr. Pimen ran into his cell and opened the eastern window, hoping to find the procession and to continue watching it, but he did not find any trace of it. The procession had vanished along with the sound he had heard.

Fr. Pimen picked up a pen and wrote down on a paper the date on which he saw the great procession. A few days later, news reached the monastery of the departure of Fr. Yostos of Abba Anthony[52]. When he asked about the day of his departure, he was told it was on the same day Fr. Pimen saw the heavenly procession. The procession was parading Fr. Yostos of Abba Anthony among Natron Valley[53] monasteries which he had not visited at all during his life.

---

52 Fr. Yostos el-Antony.
53 Wadi el-Natrun.

Receiving Communion from the Hand of Pope Kyrillos

> "Blessed be the God and Father of our Lord Jesus Christ, the Father of mercies and God of all comfort, who comforts us in all our tribulation, that we may be able to comfort those who are in any trouble."[54]

Our tender-hearted God always transforms the tribulation which He permits upon His children, into consolation and a blessing for them. The greater the tribulation is, the greater is the consolation and blessing, "for as the sufferings of Christ abound in us, so our consolation also abounds through Christ."[55] Therefore, our fathers the saints were joyful in tribulations and sorrows, and they considered them gifts from God, as the Apostle said, "for you it has been granted on behalf of Christ, not only to believe in Him, but also to suffer for His sake."[56] It is through tribulations that a man can see God, for without the tribulation through which the three youths had passed, they would not have seen God in their midst, nor enjoyed Him. So it was with Daniel the prophet and all the saints.

Here, we recount one of the tribulations that Fr. Pimen went through, which God turned into a great consolation for him. The latter he would not have dreamed of attaining without tribulation.

Fr. Pimen was accustomed to annually attend the Divine Liturgy and partake of the Holy Mysteries on the commemoration day of the departure of Pope Kyrillos VI, which is on the 9th of March. Even before he was ordained priest, he was diligent in doing this. On

---

54   2 Corinthians 1:3–4.
55   2 Corinthians 1:5.
56   Philippians 1:29.

one of the annual commemorations of Pope Kyrillos' departure, the turn fell on him to officiate the Divine Liturgy on this same day. This was a cause of great joy for Fr. Pimen.

However, the enemy of good wanted to cloud the air and to rob Fr. Pimen of this joy, so he created an unexpected problem. It happened that while Fr. Pimen was in Church during Midnight Praises service, right before the Liturgy which he was to officiate, the father responsible for distributing [the services for] the daily Liturgies[57] informed Fr. Pimen that another monk, and not him, was to officiate the Liturgy on that day.

Fr. Pimen was troubled when the father told him this news, and he returned to his cell, shutting himself in. But our tender-hearted God could not bear seeing his son in this tribulation. Therefore, He let him see a beautiful vision, consoling him in his tribulation. I leave him to relate to you, my dear reader, this vision:

> I looked, and behold, I was in the Church of Pope Benjamin the 82nd. This Church is located on the northern side of the first chorus of the ancient Church in Abba Pishoy monastery, behind the relics' cabinet containing the relics of Abba Pishoy and Abba Paul of Tamoh. I saw H.H. Pope Kyrillos VI praying the Liturgy in the Church. Praying with him was one of the bishops who is still alive. I was standing in the back of the Church, listening to the prayers of the Liturgy. Suddenly Pope Kyrillos sat down in the chair inside the sanctuary, and said, "I am tired and cannot pray." The bishop went to him and began urging him for a long time to continue the Liturgy. Finally, Pope Kyrillos

---

57 That is, the father who assigns which priest is officiating the Liturgy.

obeyed and continued the Liturgy. At the end of the Liturgy, he communed me the Body, then he took the chalice and gave me the Blood. Afterwards, I found myself in my cell, and the distress, which had taken hold of me the whole day, was dispersed with this consolation which filled my heart with joy and spiritual peace.

Building a Solitary Cell

"That Your eyes may be open toward this temple night and day, toward the place of which You said, 'My name shall be there,' that You may hear the prayer which Your servant makes toward this place."[58]

The initial idea of building solitary cells inside the monastery of the Syrians arose, being born out of the fear that monks may live in caves outside the walls of the ancient monastery. Abba Theophilus the abbot was not inclined towards this direction nor did he encourage the monks of his monastery to live in caves. This was out of his superabundant love and fear for them from the dangers and violent warfare of the devils, which the monks may go through.

The execution of this idea began in 1960 when the late Abba Theophilus demolished the old building containing the monks' cells which was attached to the southern ancient wall, to build a new cells' building which currently exists.

The supervisor over the construction works in the monastery at that time was the priest-monk Fr. Antonios of the Syrians (H.H. Pope Shenouda III, may God prolong his life), who had saved the rubble of the

---

58 1 Kings 8:29.

old building, such as the stones and wood, to be reused in building and roofing the solitary cells. The first of the solitary cells, built by Fr. Antonios of the Syrians, was for Hegumen Mettaos of the Syrians, [which was completed] in August, 1960. This was followed by a second cell, a short distance away, for the Hegumen Faltaous of the Syrians. Seeing that the idea of building solitary cells for monks was successful, more solitary cells were built subsequently.

On account of the longings and aspirations of Fr. Pimen to live in a cave in the mountain, in pursuit of the solitary life, he presented this idea Abba Theophilus the abbot. However, His Grace did not encourage him to do so. Therefore, when Fr. Pimen realized this, he spoke to him about building a solitary cell in the garden of the monastery. His Grace agreed to this after he took the approval of Fr. Pimen's father of confession Abba Sarapamon, the abbot of Abba Pishoy monastery. In December 1982, Fr. Pimen began building his solitary cell behind the southern side of the ancient wall, a place

Fr. Pimen's cell

characterized by stillness and seclusion.

When the construction of the cell was finished, Fr. Pimen invited H.G. Abba Theophilus to bless it, and on the same day Fr. Pimen moved in. The cell became for him a takeoff station to new spiritual horizons. Thus, he began to shut himself in it for weeks. He then extended it to longer spans, reaching the point of shutting himself in it throughout the span of the Great Fast, during which he did not see the face of a man nor did he speak to anyone at all. Then he shut himself in through all the fasts of the Church, and whenever he desired seclusion and solitude.

Continual Giving

> "I have shown you in every way, by laboring like this, that you must support the weak. And remember the words of the Lord Jesus, that He said, 'It is more blessed to give than to receive.'"[59]

The attributes of giving, sacrifice and service were as clear in the life of the hegumen Fr. Pimen as the sun at noon is, from before he was ordained monk in the monastery of the Syrians. These attributes continued to cling to his person, and their manifestations did not part from him for a moment, even after entering the monastery and after his ordination. We do not exaggerate when we say that [after entering the monastery], his giving, sacrifice and service became more evident and cleaved all the more to his person, even becoming part of his being so that he could not live without it. Nevertheless, these attributes took a monastic direction, in agreement with the monastic [way of] life he lived in the monastery. Fr. Pimen directed these attributes in two directions. The first direction pertains to the salvation of his soul. The

---

59   Acts 20:35.

second pertains to [the salvation of] his brothers the monks, workers, and the young men in the retreat house and extended to [include] all who loved him.

In relation to the first direction in which he directed his giving, his sacrifice, and his service for the salvation of his soul, he was earnest and he struggled strenuously in fasts, prayers, prostrations, much reading, and other kinds of strenuous spiritual labors which a monk performs in his cell.

As to the second direction, it took the form of giving, sacrifice and service, with all his ability and his power of love, sacrifice and dedication to all. Examples of this are so numerous that we could not enumerate.

One of the ways of his giving, sacrifice and service he offered to his children the monks was [manifested] when some of the monks asked him to hold a weekly spiritual meeting with them to study the Holy Scriptures. They were eager to profit from his copious learning and vast holistic knowledge of the Holy Scriptures. He consented to their request and held this meeting. Although frequently the discussion continued for long hours, he was not impatient, bored nor annoyed at anyone, but on the contrary, he answered all in equanimity, wisdom, knowledge, and wondrous long-suffering.

His giving and service to young men also continued for many years and did not stop until illness severely debilitated him. He gave a weekly sermon for the young men who were on retreat, apart from meetings for confession and guidance regarding their problems, as well as with whoever from the young men needed or desired.

Until a time near his departure, we never found him tarrying on any monk or worker or visitor asking him for medical advice or for examination, or asking for a specific medication which he might have in his private medical cabinet.

Often, monks and novices used to seek his advice and his great experience in matters related to their monastic life and their relationships together within the monastic community. All who sought him left his presence relieved, joyful and in spiritual peace. I do not exaggerate in saying that his giving, service and love included also animals, birds and the plants that were around his cell, as we will see later.

Numerous Attempts to Ordain Him a Bishop

> "Therefore, brethren, be even more diligent to make your call and election sure, for if you do these things you will never stumble."[60]

It is difficult, even rare, to find someone like Fr. Pimen, copious in knowledge and [highly] educated, [both] scientifically and religiously, and of his sublime social status, who has high spirituality, equanimity and wisdom—and yet who insists on declining the bishopric.

It is no wonder that someone like him would not accept this position, for he ran away from being ordained a priest prior to this, desiring to live in the monastery as a monk only, distant from any position or authority in the Church, whatever it may be. This stance revealed nothing other than his genuine monastic purpose which did not disappear from before his eyes, not even for a moment. He performed what Abba Anthony said: "Renew your monastic vow daily;"[61] and also what Abba Arsenius said to himself: "Arseni, Arseni, meditate on

---

60 2 Peter 1:10.
61 Cf. *The Paradise of the Holy Fathers* 2, Budge A.W., trans. (London, UK: Chatto & Windus, 1907), 85.

that for the sake of which you have left."[62] Therefore, not even for a moment did he stray from the monastic path.

A short while after his ordination a monk, an offer was presented to him that he may serve in one of the Churches in America, and afterwards, he was to be ordained a bishop, but he preferred to live as a monk in the monastery. Another time, he was offered to be ordained a bishop in Africa but he was persistent in his refusal. Therefore, he was left to his desire for a time, but this was followed by other attempts to ordain him an auxiliary bishop in 1992. It happened that H.G. Abba Sarapamon, Bishop of Abba Pishoy monastery and his father of confession, visited him in his cell to propose to him the offer of his ordination, but he excused himself also. Some days later, the late H.E. Abba Domatius, metropolitan of Giza, also visited him in his cell and offered to ordain him an auxiliary bishop with him. When Metropolitan Domatius greatly pressured him and multiplied his attempts, he was embarrassed from His Eminence, and to end the meeting, he feigned consent. Therefore, Metropolitan Domatius left him and informed H.H. the Pope of Fr. Pimen's approval to be ordained an auxiliary bishop with him. After H.E. the metropolitan went back to the Diocese of Giza, H.H. the Pope sent for Fr. Pimen to meet him in the papal residence in Abba Pishoy monastery. Fr. Pimen met His Holiness and explained to him that his consent was solely due to Metropolitan Domatius' pressure and insistence, and that he had it in his heart to live his remaining days on earth in the monastery of the Syrians. After the situation became wholly clear to H.H. the Pope, he directed Fr. Pimen to go to Metropolitan Domatius; nevertheless, he may

---

62   Cf. ibid., 14.

come back [to the monastery of the Syrians] whenever he felt wearied and disconcerted.

Fr. Pimen followed the advice of H.H. Pope Shenouda and went to Metropolitan Domatius. At his arrival, a priest of one of the Churches in Giza (Fr. Andrawis Alfy from St. George in Agouza) happened to be with Metropolitan Domatius. He told us of Metropolitan Domatius' lavish reception for Fr. Pimen and how welcoming His Eminence was at meeting him in the residence of the Diocese of Giza. He even opened his private closet and asked him to go ahead and choose whatever he wanted of his personal ecclesiastic garments. This embarrassed Fr. Pimen who declined with the utmost politeness. This visit to the Diocese of Giza did not exceed five days, most of which he spent in Tamoh monastery which belonged to the Diocese of Giza. At last, he returned to his monastery.

We leave the conversation to Fr. Pimen to tell you, dear reader, of one of the times he was called for the bishopric and how he fled from them[63]. His reverence says:

> One time, they pressured me with great persistence that I may accept to be ordained a bishop, and when they importuned me the more, I had no way out before me but to run away and hide in a cave belonging to one of the fathers the monks of the monastery. I went to the monk, who owned the cave, and asked him to let me stay in it for few days. He agreed to my request, then directed me to a place near the cave where he kept the key. I left my father the monk and set out for the mountain. Arriving at the cave, I propped my staff against it and began looking

---

63   That is, from these pressuring him.

for the key in the place where the monk had kept it. When I turned around, I saw in front of me a large black snake, of the dangerous venomous kind, in the attack position. The staff was not in my hand at the time that I may hit it. Quickly, I signed myself with the sign of the cross and signed it with the sign of the cross as well. Immediately, I saw it taking the opposite direction, fleeing from me. This encouraged me to pick up my staff and run after it, but it outran me and hid in one of the holes among the rocks. Here, I realized that Divine providence had protected me and saved me from this danger which was about to cause me harm. Afterwards, I took the key from its place, opened the cave and remained there for a few days. Finally, I returned to my cell at night, and when I met my brothers the monks, I learned from them that they had given up on speaking to me about this subject, after they had learned of my running away to the mountain and of my desire of declining this position.

A Spiritual Visit in the Cell

"As Peter was coming in, Cornelius met him and fell down at his feet and worshiped him. But Peter lifted him up, saying, 'Stand up; I myself am also a man.'"[64]

One of the monks went to visit Fr. Faltaous in his cell, who was a close friend of his reverence. During the visit, Fr. Faltaous told him, "Today, my brother, I went in spirit to one of the monks and prayed with him. His face was very shining, my brother." The visiting monk questioned him about who the monk might be. Fr. Faltaous

---

64 Acts 10:25–26.

said, "Fr. Pimen, my brother, Fr. Pimen. I was in his [cell] for a whole hour, from three to four in the morning. His face was very shining, my brother." Then the monk left Fr. Faltaous' cell, and after months had passed by, he went to visit Fr. Pimen to take his blessing. During their conversation, he told him about all his conversation with Fr. Faltaous, then asked him whether what Fr. Faltaous said happened or not. Here Fr. Pimen lowered his face to the ground and told him, embarrassed that his secret was revealed, "Yes it did happen."

Regarding this story, we are not able to comment as to what had happened, but it is far better to leave it to the dear reader, in their own thoughts, to meditate on the conversation that went on between these stars. What was the spiritual work he performed that Fr. Pimen's face shone? Was it the unceasing prayer which he practiced, or the purity of heart, or his humility and love of God, or...?

A Wondrous Scene of the Face of Christ

"And the Word became flesh and dwelt among us, and we beheld His glory, the glory as of the only begotten of the Father, full of grace and truth."[65]

Fr. Pimen had a picture of Christ with the crown of thorns, and because he loved this very much and was moved by it, he hung it in his inner chamber [of his cell][66], to always look at.

When the monk who was serving[67] him noticed that he was always looking at this picture, he said to him, "This

---

65 John 1:14.
66 *Mahbasa* [in Arabic] is a monastic term for the inner chamber of the cell where the monk shuts himself in to perform his monastic canon and his spiritual strivings, that of prayer, fasting, prostrations, reading and whatnot. (Author's note).
67 That is, attending to his needs.

picture is beautiful, father." Fr. Pimen answered him and said, "Very [beautiful], and very moving, and I love it very much." The monk continued his conversation with him, meaning to encourage and comfort him, because he was going out for an operation to remove the prostate, so he said to him, "The Lord Christ is always before you, father, and He will be with you at the time of the operation." Fr. Pimen answered him, saying, "He is not only before me; He is in me and all around my cell."

On Sunday, the 3rd of September, 2005, Fr. Pimen went out to Mansoura for the second operation on the prostate, and while outside the monastery, it happened that one of the visiting youths in the monastery, as he was walking, saw Fr. Pimen's cell. Its beauty caught his attention, so he decided to take a photo of it to keep it for himself. He did not have but his cell phone's camera and he went up a high area to get a clearer view. After he took the photo, he looked at his phone's screen, and was surprised to see a picture of the face of the Lord Christ above the cell and He was looking at it. This was formed by the leaves and tree branches as they were moved by the wind, in an indescribable ingenuity and high degree of clarity, as though God were saying to the one who owns the cell, "Behold, I am with you and will keep you wherever you go,"[68] and even when you are in the operation room, My eyes are on you. With this image which was formed above Fr. Pimen's cell, God wanted to honor him, and to reveal his holiness before his departure from this world to the Excellent Glory[69]. A question remains unanswered: has Fr. Pimen seen the face of the Lord Christ looking at his cell before this photo was taken? This might be why he told the monk serving him, "He is not only before me; He is in me and all around my cell."

---

68   Genesis 28:15.
69   See: 2 Peter 1:17.

PART ONE
Father Pimen's Life

CHAPTER THREE
His Spiritual Virtues

His Spiritual Virtues

"Tell me, fathers and brothers, where did our fathers acquire the virtues: in the world or in the desert? So we, how do we want to acquire virtue while we are in the world? If we do not hunger, do not thirst, do not shiver with cold, do not dwell with wild beasts and do not die in the body, how can we live in the soul?"[70]

—Abba Macarius the Great—

The power in these timeless words which Abba Macarius uttered lies in [the fact] that he actually lived them. Many [church] servants have spoken about virtue and taught it but could not live it. Even those who were capable of living it, could not live it to perfection, but only partially. There are many virtues which are difficult for people living in the world to practice, such as silence, unceasing prayer, and stillness. Even though they may practice these virtues while living in the world, they could not practice them except to imperfectly. The reason for this does not lie in them themselves but due to the numerous hindrances and offences which defile the soul, to which they are exposed directly or indirectly in the world.

Therefore, the lovers of virtue endeavored to depart from the world and go into the wilderness, for they had the confidence and certainty that the wilderness was the most favorable and suitable place to acquire virtues.

Dr. Wadih Ameen was one of these who left the world with all its glories and went to the monastery of

---

[70] *The Anonymous Sayings of the Desert Fathers*, Wortley J., trans. (Cambridge, UK: Cambridge University Press, 2013), N.764.

the Syrians, because he had the confidence and certainty that he would not attain the perfection of virtues except in the wilderness, wherein are hunger and thirst, and death of the body and living with the beasts.

Fr. Pimen lived nearly forty years in struggle and strenuous asceticism. In it, he brought forth fruit of abundant and numerous virtues. I will take you with me, dear reader, to look together over a few of these virtues and spiritual traits with which Fr. Pimen was adorned, in order that we may be comforted by them and take them as a model for us, imitating him on the path of our struggle on earth to attain the prize like him and win the eternal inheritance.

Love

"Humility is the raiment of Divinity but love is God Himself"

—Fr. Pimen—

Love is the first and the greatest among all the virtues. Christ confirmed this by saying to the Pharisee, "'You shall love the Lord your God with all your heart, with all your soul, and with all your mind.' This is the first and great commandment. And the second is like it: 'You shall love your neighbor as yourself.'"[71] St. Paul the Apostle referred to this also when he said, "And now abide faith, hope, love, these three; but the greatest of these is love."[72]

The roots of love, which ran deep and were embedded in the heart of Fr. Pimen, go back to many years past, beginning from [the time] when he was still a boy, since

---

71 Matthew 22:37–39.
72 1 Corinthians 13:13.

the time he started Sunday School service when he was thirteen years old to the time of his departure to the monastery of the Syrians. If love were the foundation onto which service is built, then without a doubt it was this that moved Dr. Wadih Ameen to offer, give and sacrifice. Without a doubt also, the success of his service may be attributed to the power of love burning within him and moving him [to care] for the salvation of everyone. When Dr. Wadih went to the monastery of the Syrians, becoming a monk named Fr. Pimen, he did not leave the love which was in his heart outside in the world, before coming to the monastery, but the same powerful love in his heart he brought to the monastery of the Syrians. This love however, having the same strength, was transformed into love for God and love for neighbor. In other words, it was transformed in a monastic direction, suitable with the new [way of] life he pursued. Therefore, we found Fr. Pimen, once [he was ordained] monk, that his powerful love in his heart began to move him toward mighty strivings and assiduous activity in prayers, fasting, prostrations and other strivings which revealed his love for God.

On the other hand, love began to move him to serve his brothers the monks in the monastery of the Syrians, Abba Pishoy and Baramos monasteries, the workers of the monastery, visitors and every person he felt was in need of his help. So as not to make it too long, dear reader, I will present to you nuggets out of numerous instances with Fr. Pimen, that you may see with me how powerful and overflowing his love was to all without exception.

Fr. Paphnotius of the Syrians (H.G. Abba Mettaos, abbot of the monastery of the Syrians) used to suffer from an infection, which recurred very often, and he used to treat it with Sefagen injections. It happened that one day, he suffered from that recurrent infection, and out of his abundant humility and ample politeness, not wanting to disturb Fr. Pimen by going to him for the injection, which he always needed for the treatment of the infection, he found one last injection of this kind in his cell, but it was expired and he did not know it.

He took it and asked the monk who was living near him to administer it to him. A few minutes later, signs of an allergic reaction appeared on him and he began to tremble greatly, his heart beat faster, and he felt at that moment that he was giving up the spirit. When the fathers around him saw this, they hastened to Fr. Pimen, and explained to him Fr. Paphnotius' condition. Fr. Pimen, then, took an injection from his cell and quickly went to Fr. Paphnotius and administered it to him. A little later, Fr. Paphnotius felt discernibly better after Fr. Pimen had saved him from a sure death. As the Book says, "Love never fails."[73] Therefore, whenever [the name of] Fr. Pimen was brought up in conversation, H.G. Abba Mettaos would mention this love which saved him from death.

Here, we remember another instance which is very similar to the previous one. A long time ago, the custom was that a group of monks of the monastery of the Syrians would gather in the evening of Resurrection Sunday every year, to prepare colored eggs, *fesikh*[74], scallions and meat. This was done in preparation for the following day, that is, Sham Ennessim[75], when H.H. Pope Shenouda III comes to the monastery of the Syrians and meets, in the garden of the monastery, the fathers the bishops and monks of the other monasteries

---

73   1 Corinthians 13:8.
74   Fermented salted fish.
75   This is an Egyptian national festival, which always falls on Easter Monday.

(those of Abba Pishoy, Baramos, and St. Mina), and also the monks of the monastery of the Syrians. And they would eat the meal together.

Fr. Pimen was one of the main fathers who participated every year in the preparation of food for this day. Of those participating in the preparation was an ascetic monk who would fast for days [without eating], abstaining from [the time after] the Liturgy of Covenant Thursday to the glorious Feast of the Resurrection. One time, after putting great efforts in preparing the food, the monk could not continue working and his strength failed him and he, pale, fainted to the ground, nearly taking his last breath. When Fr. Pimen saw what had happened, he ran to give him first aid. The monk, who was lying on the ground, looked at him and said, "Do not bother yourself. I'm dying, this is it. I know that; I am a doctor." Fr. Pimen quickly got up and ran towards the building of the cells in the ancient monastery. He leaped up the stairs quickly until he reached the clinic on the fourth floor. He took an injection which was before him, as if God had prepared it for him, and came in haste down to the monk and administered the injection to him. A little later the sick monk regained his consciousness. He, then, was given some medications and supplements until he regained his health completely. All the monks felt, at this time, God's powerful work who saved their brother the monk who fell ill, and also [felt] the powerful love that Fr. Pimen showed towards his brothers the monks in the monastery of the Syrians.

There are other occurrences similar to what we have already mentioned, revealing the love Fr. Pimen had for his brothers the monks and for everyone. These you will encounter intertwined with the virtue of giving and his other virtues, about which we will speak.

His love for God, however, you will find clearly manifested when we speak of unceasing prayer, seriousness and commitment, silence, purity of heart, and other virtues.

Overall, we may say that the virtue of love was intertwined with, and manifest in Fr. Pimen's conduct and life.

> *"True love that is from God wins all, even the enemies."*
> —Fr. Pimen—

Prayer

> *"Go out with Him into the wilderness and ascend with Him the mountains and sit quietly down at His feet with the beasts which came to be comforted by their Lord. And there, arise with Him to learn warfare and fighting with the enemies."*
> —The Spiritual Elder—

Going Out to the Mountain for Prayer

How beautiful what the Bible said of the Lord Christ:

"And everyone went to his own house. But Jesus went to the Mount of Olives."[76]

And verses carrying the same meaning frequently appear [in the Bible], such as:

---

76 John 7:53–8:1.

"And when He had sent the multitudes away, He went up on the mountain by Himself to pray. Now when evening came, He was alone there."[77]

"And when He had sent them away, He departed to the mountain to pray."[78]

"Now it came to pass in those days that He went out to the mountain to pray, and continued all night in prayer to God."[79]

"And in the daytime He was teaching in the temple, but at night He went out and stayed on the mountain called Olivet."[80]

In many things, we find the son imitating his father, and the father rejoices in his son when he sees him doing that. So did Fr. Pimen imitate his heavenly Father and learned from Him to go to the mountain to spend the whole night in unceasing prayer and constant cleaving to God. In a previous chapter, we mentioned how ardently Fr. Pimen loved going out to the wilderness, there spending the whole night in prayer.

Unceasing Prayer

How beautiful is the saying of Abba Anthony, the father of monks, on the Jesus Prayer: "Abandon not the name

---

[77] Matthew 14:23.
[78] Mark 6:46.
[79] Luke 6:12.
[80] Luke 21:37.

of the Lord Jesus, but hold[81] it with your mind and sing it with your tongue and in your heart."[82] This saying truly fits Fr. Pimen who practiced[83] the Jesus Prayer even until his heart became inflamed with God and until his mind continually cleaved to God. He often even forgot to eat and drink, and sometimes did not hear nor realize the presence of those near him. About the latter, one of the fathers the monks told us that one day, he went to Fr. Pimen's cell and knocked persistently on his door. Fr. Pimen, however, out of his constant occupation with prayer to God, was unaware and did not hear the knocking on the door, until the cat, which was in his cell, came to him and began pulling his clothes with its mouth and pawing his foot. Only then did Fr. Pimen realize and went to open the door for the monk, after a long time had passed.

Another monk, one of the fathers serving him during his illness, related that in the span of a single night, he went to Fr. Pimen three times, and every time, he found Fr. Pimen sitting on a chair inside the inner chamber of his cell[84], muttering words with his mouth, in such a deep strong prayer that he did not sense his presence nor was he aware of his entrance, him approaching, and not even when he stood beside him and called him. This is how Fr. Pimen prayed. There is another story revealing to us the life of unceasing prayer that Fr. Pimen lived.

We mentioned previously that the late Abba Theophilus, the abbot of the monastery of the Syrians

---

81 See Song of Songs 3:4.
82 The saying continues as follows: "… and say, 'My Lord Jesus Christ have mercy on me; my Lord Jesus Christ, help me.' Also say, 'I praise You, my Lord Jesus Christ.'" *Bostan Al-Rohban Al-Mowasah, Al-joz' Al-Awal* [The Expanded Paradise of the Monks, Part 1]. (Egypt: St. Macarius Monastery, 2006), 45.
83 Literally: mastered.
84 Arabic: *mahbasa*.

had permitted Fr. Pimen to bring his private car with him when he came seeking monasticism, that it may be of help to him in his movements among the monasteries for the treatment of patients, or may help him fulfill some of the monastery's needs.

One day, Fr. Pimen went by car to one of the garages in the rest house area to fix the radiator. When Fr. Pimen learned that fixing it would take three to four hours, he took a chair, sat in a quiet area and began praying the Jesus Prayer. During this [time], the car of the monastery of the Syrians was coming back [to the monastery], bringing Fr. Faltaous back, and when it came near Fr. Pimen, the car stopped. Fr. Faltaous put his head out of the car window and said to Fr. Pimen, "Remember me, remember me, my brother." He, then, continued on his way. When Fr. Pimen returned to the monastery of the Syrians, he met Fr. Faltaous and asked him for the reason of him speaking to him that way after the car had stopped at the garage. Fr. Faltaous answered him saying, "You see, my brother, angels were all around you and were joyful and rejoicing. This is why, my brother, I told you, 'Remember me.'"

Fr. Pimen remained silent and did not say a word, after God had revealed to Fr. Faltaous what Fr. Pimen was doing at that time: Unceasing prayer and reciting the name of Jesus.

Spiritual Watchfulness

Fr. Pimen lived the saying of the Lord Christ: "And what I say to you, I say to all: Watch!"[85]

Fr. Pimen lived in the same manner as the great fathers of monasticism, keeping vigil[86] all night long

---

85   Mark 13:37.
86   Also: watch.

until dawn, and afterwards, he would lay down a little to rest. He used to spend most of the night in unceasing prayer, after the example of Abba Arsenius who would stand for prayer at sunset, leaving the sun behind him, and continued in prayer all night long until the sun rose before him;[87] and also after the manner of Sts. Maximus and Dometius whom St. Macarius the Great saw keeping vigil all night long in prayer, and when morning came, they pretended to be sleeping so that St. Macarius might not know of their watchfulness and their all-night prayer.[88]

Fr. Pimen loved keeping vigil throughout his life until he passed away. This practice was known and common among the fathers the monks of the monastery of the Syrians.

We learned that Fr. Pimen had practiced[89] the life of prayer through three main means: going out to the mountain for prayer, unceasing prayer which he would constantly recite, and keeping vigil in prayer all night long.

---

87   See *The Paradise of the Holy Fathers* 2, Budge A.W., trans. (London, UK: Chatto & Windus, 1907), 24.
88   See *The Paradise of the Holy Fathers* 1, Budge A.W., trans. (London, UK: Chatto & Windus, 1907), 240–242.
89   Literally: mastered.

Giving

"The class of monks is a class of toilers, giving its fruit to the Church, the world, and the service. As much as possible, the monk must keep secret his activities and his inner strivings, and every activity or service he offers must not be internalized."

—Fr. Pimen—

The virtue of giving is one of the greatest virtues in Christianity, and Christ and His Apostles frequently pointed to it in their conversations and teachings to the people. Christ said: "But rather give alms of such things as you have."[90] But He went a step higher than this, and said, "Sell what you have and give alms."[91]

The virtue of giving should not be limited to the giving of material things only, such as [giving] money to those in need, or giving food, drink, clothing, and the like. Instead, we ought to rise above in our giving until we reach the giving of spiritual things, wherein a man gives his body, his soul and his spirit to God and also to others. The Holy Scriptures pointed to this, saying: "Greater love has no one than this, than to lay down one's life for his friends."[92] Both [types of] giving, of material and spiritual things, should include giving to God and giving also to others. Giving to God is not by giving tithes, giving first fruits, giving vows and other kinds of giving, but should be a spiritual [kind of] giving, wherein a man gives his whole soul, body and spirit, to God. Giving to others is not only that of the

---

90 Luke 11:41.
91 Luke 12:33.
92 John 15:13.

material aid (money, food, and clothing), but it should also include giving the soul, body and spirit for the sake of others.

It was clear and evident, before all, that the virtue of giving was the adornment of the life and conduct of Fr. Pimen. Regarding his giving to God, it was not limited to giving donations and aids, but he rose above [this] in that he gave his soul, his body, and his spirit to God, when he consecrated his whole life to God, becoming a monk in the monastery of the Syrians. He joined the hosts of the earthly angels who say to God at all times, "For Your sake we are killed all day long."[93]

We cannot enumerate [all] the spiritual offerings which Fr. Pimen gave God—how many prayers, fasts, prostrations, works of mercy, works of love, service he offered to God with indescribable love and joy.

As to Fr. Pimen's giving to others, it was a continual giving to his children and his brothers the monks. He would often buy for them blankets, shoes, food, fruits, fabric to make cassocks for the monks, and other similar things he offered to the monastery that they may be distributed to the monks. Many trusted in him and had a great bond of love with him. From time to time, they used to ask for his opinion about how they may spend their tithes, and he would advise them to give part of it to the monks in a tangible manner. Others would give him the money and entrust him with buying whatever he finds suitable for his children the monks. Fr. Pimen took care of buying and distributing [to the monks], and this work made him very happy because of his exceedingly great love for them.

His giving was not only limited to monks, but also included the workers of the monastery. Often, he would

---

93   Romans 8:36.

buy for them meat and vegetables, would cook it himself in his cell, and then would take it in his car to el-Dawar, the place where workers are. He would give it to the man in charge of the workers, to distribute it to them. This work he did in the utmost joy and happiness. Out of his exceeding humility, Fr. Pimen would not send for the person in charge of preparing food for the workers, to come and pick up the food he made for them from his cell, but instead would carry it himself and deliver it to them.

The virtue of giving occupied a large portion of Fr. Pimen's being and heart, so much so that he gave to everyone, as long as he was able to give. Therefore, his giving did not stop at people only but included animals, birds, and plants also. We found him many times, while he was eating, putting aside a portion from what he was eating to give to the cats and dogs, and often, he would place the leftover food, such as bread and rice, on the fence outside his cell so that when the birds—pigeons, doves and sparrows—come, they may find their food. Likewise, he cared for the trees that are planted around his cell, giving them fertilizer and water, and spraying them with pesticide, so that they may flower and produce good fruit.

With all these types of giving, we should not forget his spiritual giving to every soul coming to him, in distress, sorrow or despair. How many living words, full of comfort, encouragement and hope, did he give to these souls, so that they left him full of hope, joy, peace and calmness. The more he took from God in his prayers and in his relationship with Him, the more he offered to all these souls, generously, [both] comfort and hope.

Humility and Self-Denial

"The person who attains true humility, wins all people and wins all hearts, with the grace of our Lord Jesus Christ"

—Fr. Pimen—

Humility is the virtue that reveals the children of God and distinguishes them from among the children of the world. For He said, "Learn from Me, for I am gentle and lowly in heart, and you will find rest for your souls."[94]

The true humility and gentleness which Fr. Pimen possessed[95], made him a living icon of the Lord Christ. His humility was not external humility, springing from external appearances, but it was a humility that sprang from the inward depths of his heart and overflowed outwardly. Therefore, every person who dealt with him or beheld him, beheld in him the image of the Lord Christ.

The saintly fathers say, "The humble heart is a place for the dwelling of God." The true humility which Fr. Pimen lived, made his heart a dwelling of God, and here lies the hidden power which brought forth a mighty spiritual power coming out of him.

Of the important and clear signs indicating the humility of Fr. Pimen was his self-denial and his fleeing from vainglory. For the latter's sake, he persisted in running away for five years from Abba Theophilus, the abbot of the monastery, so that he may not place his hand on him, thus ordaining him a priest. His running away was out of feeling unworthy of this priestly order, this feeling certainly indicating his true humility. On

---

94 Matthew 11:29.
95 Literally: lived.

the other hand, his running away was [also] out of his fear lest he be chosen and called to serve in the world. This also comes back to his true humility, in feeling that he was weak.

In self-denial and fleeing from vainglory, he ran away from being ordained a bishop as we have mentioned previously. Running away from this and that, is an absolute proof of his true humility, for had his humility been only external, he would not have been able to resist the temptations of vainglory and self-parading which the human soul seeks.

Of the clear signs revealing the humility of Fr. Pimen is that he did not boast of his wealth and social status which he enjoyed before his ordination a monk in the monastery of the Syrians. Also, he did not show off nor boast of his knowledge and education, whether [his] spiritual, religious education or his worldly, scientific education.

It is not easy for a person who is a teacher, a mentor and a servant to give up this position, becoming a disciple, a trainee and receiving monastic guidance. The humility of Fr. Pimen, however, made him give up his position and status as a teacher, mentor and servant, which had weightiness in the world, and go to the monastery, thereby becoming a disciple, training in virtues, and learning the spiritual and monastic tenets from those who might be less knowledgeable and less learned than him.

The acceptance of Fr. Pimen to give up his job as a skilled and successful surgeon with fame and status; and to give up his position as a successful and well-known servant with many spiritual children—that he may go to the monastery, a place devoid of all this glory and spotlight, to bury himself and his honor, and to become a nobody—this is a proof of his heart's true humility.

> *"Seek true humility from Christ Himself, for He is the God of humility and the humble"*
> —Fr. Pimen—

A wonderful story comes to my mind which reveals Fr. Pimen's humility, which was told by one of the monks of the monastery of the Syrians.

It happened that Fr. Pimen suffered from sharp pain in the vertebrae of his vertebral column, and in these days he used to go to the hospital for treatment. One of his children, a servant [in church], went to [visit] him and urged him to give a talk in their Church meeting. Though Fr. Pimen tried to excuse himself, it was to no avail before this servant's insistence and importunity. Therefore, Fr. Pimen consented to attending and prepared gifts that he may give to them at the end of the meeting.

During this meeting, a disagreement broke between this servant and the one in charge of the meeting about their viewpoints on the gifts. When the servant went back to Fr. Pimen, he was surprised by what Fr. Pimen said to him: "What's wrong, my son? Tell me and I will give you rest." The servant denied there being anything, but Fr. Pimen repeated to him the same words. Therefore, the servant related to him the whole affair, amazed at Fr. Pimen's clairvoyance.

Fr. Pimen, then, took his cane on which he was leaning with one hand, and with the other hand, he leaned on the servant, since at that time he had great difficulty walking. When he came to the person who was in charge, though he could not, he made a prostration to him, even until touching the ground with his hand. He said, "I have sinned, forgive me. I did not know this would upset you."

Before the humility of this elder, the person in charge was greatly ashamed and began asking for Fr. Pimen's absolution and forgiveness, keeping in mind the great difference in age between Fr. Pimen and the servant in charge of the meeting. By his humility, the problem was resolved.

Therefore, we trust that God will never forget Fr. Pimen's humility, his self-denial and his fleeing from vainglory while on earth. He will reveal him in the last day and crown him with the most radiant glory which is incorruptible and undefiled and that does not fade away, in heaven.[96]

"Love and humility destroy malice and pride, and win souls to God."
—Fr. Pimen—

Seriousness and Commitment

"Spiritual gifts are given for free by God; virtues, however, come through striving."
—Fr. Pimen—

One of the things demanded of a Christian is to be serious and committed in all matters of their life, and especially in their relationship with God. What benefit is it that a man builds today but demolishes tomorrow, or that he plants today but uproots tomorrow? If the

---

96 Cf. 1 Peter 1:4.

person is not serious and committed in his life, without a doubt, he will fall back and regress little by little until he fails in all matters of his life. Likewise, every Christian ought to be serious and committed in his spiritual life so that he could succeed in it and could build and grow it in the Lord.

If this were the case for the layperson living in the world, how much more is it for the monk who is standing at all times in the arena of striving against Satan and his soldiers. It is very important and necessary for a monk to live all his life in seriousness and commitment lest he be in travails on the road of perfection in which he presses that he may come to the stature of the fullness of Christ.[97]

Seriousness and commitment are the most important traits distinguishing the life of Fr. Pimen, from the first day he entered the monastery of the Syrians. They were not new things added to his character in his new monastic life, but rather were clear traits in his earlier life before entering the monastery. Had he not been serious and committed in it, he would not have been successful as he joined medical school and graduated from it a skillful surgeon; and had he not been serious and committed, he would not have been successful in his work and also he would not have been successful in his service which grew to reach many cities; nor would he have been able to continue in Sunday School service for thirty years without interruption.

Therefore, seriousness and commitment were clearly manifest in Fr. Pimen's monastic and spiritual life, in his relationship with his brothers the monks, and in every work he was entrusted with by the monastery's management.

---

97 Ephesians 4:13.

Regarding his monastic striving, he was serious and committed in his fasts in which he abstained from food for long intervals; in his prayers also in which he gradually progressed until he reached high degrees such as rumination[98] and cleaving to God. Had he not been serious and committed, he would not have attained the Jesus Prayer and ceaseless rumination[99] in prayer, because such virtues require from the monk great striving, extreme concentration, and ceaseless watchfulness, in order to practice and acquire them.

Of the signs revealing Fr. Pimen's seriousness and commitment which were clear in his labors, is the constant seclusion in the cell. He lived as a monk who shut himself in his solitary cell for long intervals, especially during fasting periods. During the Great Fast, for example, he did not leave his cell at all; therefore, he spoke to no one and did not see the face of a man during this time which spans over a month and a half. We do not know, my dear reader, what fierce spiritual practices he did during this period inside his cell, that of prayers, fasts, prostrations, reading.

Fr. Pimen was also committed and observant of the monastery's rules and was submissive to its regulation. He performed them with all exactness, and without haughtiness, obstinacy, or objecting to them. For example, when he was in need of going out of the monastery for treatment or to fulfill some personal affairs, he never went out except after taking permission from the abbot of the monastery, regardless of his old age and his having spent many years in monasticism. This was before illness vehemently attacked him, hindering him from walking and moving.

---

98   The Arabic word is *hatheeth*, which may be translated to "meditation."
99   Arabic: *hatheeth*.

Fr. Pimen was also serious and committed in his minute observance of the monastic principles, such as not going out into the world except for treatment or for carrying out necessary affairs and needs, and the latter would occur [only] rarely. He was also observant of avoiding too much mingling with laypeople, eager to preserve his monastic life, lest he slide into the abyss of these dangers, thereby losing his life as a monk.

Silence

"He who speaks in a godly manner does well; he who remains silent in the same way, likewise."[100]

—Abba Pimen[101] the Solitary—

Many are the verses in the Holy Scriptures and numerous the sayings of the holy fathers, which abundantly speak of the danger of speaking and the importance of the virtue of silence. If speaking has its danger within a community outside [the monastery], then its danger and harm are all the more serious within the monastic community. This is because the community in the monastery is a closed community. Therefore, the saintly fathers practiced the virtue of silence, lest an unprofitable or harmful word escapes their mouth, thereby hurting its hearer. This is on the negative side. As for the positive side, [they remained silent] so that their talking to people may not keep them away from talking to God. Therefore, silence provides an opportunity for them to pray or ruminate[102], to meditate or read the word of God. For all this, Fr. Pimen loved silence, speaking

---

100 *Give Me a Word: The Alphabetical Sayings of the Desert Fathers*, Wortley J., trans. (Yonkers, NY: SVS Press, 2014), Poemen 146.
101 Spelled "Poemen" in the Paradise of the Holy Fathers.
102 Arabic: *hatheeth*.

but a little, and frequently he used to sit in silence until someone asked him a question. He would, then, answer him with brevity so great that one of the fathers said about him, "Fr. Pimen's silence is comforting." Perhaps he remained silent to preserve himself from speaking, keeping before himself the saying of the Book, "He who guards his mouth preserves his life"[103]; "Whoever guards his mouth and tongue keeps his soul from troubles"[104].

St. Isaac the Syrian says, "If you want to know who a man of God is, let his constant silence inform you." As to the main reason for which Fr. Pimen remained silent, it is his ceaseless occupation with conversing with God, in meditating on the name of Salvation of our Lord Jesus Christ[105]. Through ceaseless conversing with God, a feeling of indescribable spiritual delight was born in him, thereby stimulating him all the more to remain silent.

There are many factors that helped Fr. Pimen to obtain the virtue of silence, namely, living in a solitary cell, remote from excessive mingling with the monks in the monastic community, and adding to this his seclusion in his cell for long intervals, especially during the Great Fast.

---

103 Proverbs 13:3.
104 Proverbs 21:23.
105 See Sunday Theotokia Part I.

Purity of Heart

One time, St. Isaac the Syrian was asked about what purity of soul is. He answered, saying, "It is a heart that shows mercy to all created nature."[106] Another asked him, saying, "What is a merciful heart?" He answered, [saying], "It is the heart's burning for the sake of the entire creation, for men, for birds, for animals, ..., and for every created thing; and at the recollection and sight of them, the eyes of a merciful man pour forth abundant tears. From the strong and vehement mercy that grips his heart and from his great compassion, his heart is humbled and he cannot bear to hear or to see any injury or slight sorrow in creation."[107]

All the words of St. Isaac the Syrian can be truly applied to Fr. Pimen. All the monks and all who have had interactions with him testify of his tenderness and compassion with which he treated every patient coming to him, whether he is a monk or a worker. Regarding this tenderness and compassion, which reveal Fr. Pimen's purity of heart, we will mention the following story.

It happened that one of the workers, while asleep, was stung by a scorpion in the middle of the night, and was awakened from sleep out of pain. On seeing this, his fellow workers called in haste the monk responsible for them. He came to them and quickly carried the worker to Fr. Pimen. After examining him and treating him, the monk [who brought the worker] persisted in thanking Fr. Pimen for what he did for him and he apologized for coming to him at such a late hour of the night. But Fr. Pimen, in love, mercy and tenderness, assured them and asked them to come to him whenever the patient felt

---

106 Cf. *The Ascetical Homilies of Saint Isaac the Syrian.* (Boston, MA: Holy Transfiguration Monastery, 2011), 491.
107 Ibid.

pain. The monk with the workers left, marveling at the purity of Fr. Pimen's heart.

Also, out of the purity of Fr. Pimen's heart, he was pained to see a dog or cat or any other animal suffering from hunger. He would readily have pity on them and have compassion on them by giving them food.

He would also moisten fragments of bread with water and place them outside, on top of his cell's fence, for sparrows, pigeons and birds to eat. Even trees won his compassion and pity, for he used to take care of them and water them.

Fr. Pimen's heart was devoid of any grudges, hatred, jealousy or any evil whatsoever against a monk or layperson, confirming the purity of his heart. What we have seen and handled of the love in his heart toward all is a sure sign of the purity of his heart.

PART ONE

Father Pimen's Life

CHAPTER FOUR

His Relationship with the Saints

His Relationship with the Saints

The relationship between a person and others has great importance, for on its basis a person's personality is shaped. Therefore, a person's relationship with good people helps him do good, and positively impacts his personality. In contrast, a person's relationship with bad people drives him to bad conduct. Of this the Holy Scripture warns us, saying, "Evil company corrupts good habits."[108]

Regarding this, one of the desert fathers said, "If a diligent person lives with those who are not diligent, he does not make any progress. But he can still struggle so as not to fall behind. But if a lazy person lives with those who are diligent, he will make progress if he is vigilant."[109]

Since the time Dr. Wadih Ameen was a young man, he took for himself spiritual fathers and friends, and clung to them. As a result, they lifted him up to high spiritual levels, making him praise in high heavenly horizons with the ranks of angels and saints. There is no doubt that Dr. Wadih's close company with these spiritual [fathers and friends] had its powerful and effectual impact on shaping his personality. This had overloaded him with experience and shrewdness in his spiritual and practical life. This was felt by all who interacted with him.

Of the very clear things, with which Dr. Wadih was distinguished, was his tireless pursuit and his searching for contemporary saints, and working at forming a relationship with them. This, my dear reader, is what you will be reading in the following pages.

---

108   1 Corinthians 15:33.
109   *The Sayings of the Desert Fathers: The Systematic Collection*, Baker B., trans. (Florence, AZ: SAGOM Press, 2019), 133.

His Relationship with [Contemporary] Saints Before Their Departure

"If you fall short of being rich in God, then cling to the one who is rich in Him, that you may be happy through his happiness, and that you may learn how to walk according to the commandments of the Scriptures. So if you love the pure, they will be your friends, and with them you will reach the City of God which is full of light."

—Abba Pachomius the Great—

Fr. Mina The Solitary (H.H. Pope Kyrillos VI)

The young man Wadih Ameen had known Fr. Mina the Solitary since 1948 when he was 19 years old and still a student in medical school. Fr. Pimen related to us the story of how his relationship with Fr. Mina the Solitary began and how it progressed. His reverence says:

> One day while I was at church, I heard that a group from the congregation of the church would be attending the Vespers Raising of Incense at St. Mina's Church in El-Zahraa with Fr. Mina the Solitary. I had not heard of him before, so I decided to go with them to take the blessing of Fr. Mina and meet him.
>
> After finishing the Vespers prayer, we met Fr. Mina and I

asked him to become my father of confession, especially after I revealed to him my monastic yearnings. Since that day in 1948 my relationship with him continued, as my father of confession, until 1959 when he became the Patriarch, with the name Pope Kyrillos VI. After this, he apologized to me and said, "Look for another father of confession for yourself, because I can't follow up on you, with the affairs of the Patriarchate." So I took his blessing and left. Afterwards, I followed his advice and took Fr. Mikhael Ibrahim as my father of confession [lasting] until the time I left to the monastery of the Syrians in 1972.

And Fr. Pimen continues to recount the story of his relationship with Fr. Mina the Solitary, saying:

After the departure of Pope Yousab II, nominations for the Patriarch began. The Chief Committee of Sunday School submitted three nominations from its children, to fill this supreme position. And they were:

1. The monk Makari of the Syrians (the late Abba Samuel, Bishop of General Services).
2. The monk Antonios of the Syrians (H.H. Pope Shenouda III, may God prolong his life).
3. The monk Matthew the Poor, of the Syrians

When Mr. Waheeb Atta-Allah (Later, the late His Grace Bishop Gregorios), who was a member of the Chief Committee of Sunday School, saw that the Committee did not nominate him along with the candidates, he left it and joined the Friends of the Holy Bible Association.

The Association then nominated him for the Patriarchate while he was still a layperson.

The electoral campaign began by making and distributing pamphlets, and we were young men with enthusiasm and fiery zeal, especially because the three candidates from Sunday School were our fellows prior to becoming monks.

During that time, I went to Fr. Mina the Solitary for confession, and at the end of the confession session, he said to me, "What's this you're doing; it is wrong. You ought to nominate someone greater than you, to be a transitional stage. Afterwards he will take you and ordain all of you."

After Fr. Mina the Solitary finished talking, I looked at his face. It was beaming a marvelous light, and I thought, "You are the man." I found him looking at me searchingly, suggesting that he realized what I was saying in my heart.

What he revealed to me truly came to pass. That is, the altar lot fell on him and he became the Pope of the Church, named Pope Kyrillos VI. He ordained many of Sunday School servants bishops and priests for the service of evangelism.

Fr. Pimen continues his conversation about his memories of Fr. Mina the Solitary, saying:

> I went to Fr. Mina the Solitary at St. Mina's Church in El-Zahraa. Coincidentally, it was on that day that the result of the altar lot was to be revealed, announcing who would be the Pope of the Church.
>
> After I attended Liturgy and partook of the

Communion, I stood before the sanctuary talking with Fr. Mina the Solitary. As we were conversing together, a woman came in through the door of the church, crying out, saying, "Congratulation Fr. Mina! Your Reverence will be the Pope. The lot came out with your name." We all stood still and were stunned and delighted at the news we heard. We saw Fr. Mina quickly enter the sanctuary, and he cried out three times audibly, saying, "If You have commanded, then You will help me." Then he came out of the sanctuary, tears filling his eyes. He was crying bitterly, and people began coming in to congratulate him regarding this position.

Such was the relationship between Fr. Pimen (Dr. Wadih Ameen) and Fr. Mina the Solitary, a very strong and very firm relationship. Fr. Pimen expressed it in simple yet meaningful words, saying, "The first day that I met Fr. Mina the Solitary, I found what I was looking for in him."

Father Abdel Messih of Manahra

Dr. Wadih Ameen was like a bee gathering nectar from among the flowers. This is how he endeavored to search for spiritual fathers, to rejoice at meeting them and take their blessing.

Fr. Abdel Messih of St. Macarius, known as of Manahra, was one of these [fathers] whose name was imprinted in the horizons and was on the lips of many. When Dr. Wadih heard the news and stories of the holiness of Fr. Abdel Messih of Manahra, he set out on a long journey in search of him, and he finally won the blessing of seeing and meeting him. I leave you, my dear reader, with Fr. Pimen to tell you about his fortitude and his long-suffering, and the pains he went through until this meeting with Fr. Abdel Messih took place. And his reverence says:

> I remained a long time in search of Fr. Abdel Messih of Manahra and his whereabouts. In one of the two-week conferences for the Sunday School servants in Alexandria on the level of the government, I met a servant—who afterwards became a monk. When I asked him about Fr. Abdel Messih, he told me that he knew him well because he lived in his town. He showed readiness to go with me to visit him.
>
> On an appointed day, I went to Fadimin village in Faiyum. The servant picked me up and we went together to Bosh, and there we met Fr. Abdel Messih of Abba Paul in the residence of the monastery of Abba Paul. He is Fr. Fanous of Abba Paul's brother in monasticism. I informed my friend that this was not he of whom I had spoken, but regardless, we took his blessing and left.
>
> After I returned to my town in peace, I scrupulously asked about Fr. Abdel Messih of St. Macarius and I was told he was in Manahra village. When I was determined on going to him, I went first to Manahra village and asked about him and some of the loving people who lived in the village guided me to the hut where Fr. Abdel Messih lived. It was located about a kilometer and a half away from the village. I found his room to be very small, its walls made of mud, its roof of palm leaves. When I arrived I found

its door open and Fr. Abdel Messih was sitting on the ground inside. I went in and greeted him, then I sat down in front of him on the ground; however, I could not open my mouth and say a word to him. After a long time had passed in silence, he said to me, "What do you want, you brother? And why are you sitting like this?" I said, "I want a blessing from you." He, then, rebuked me and said to me, "What blessing, what blessing! Get out of here, get out of here." So I went out and sat down on the ground beside the door, and said to myself, "Do I, after looking for him all these months, leave easily?"

As I was sitting beside the door, some of the passersby saw me, so they gathered around me and told me of some miracles Fr. Abdel Messih had performed. After fifteen minutes had gone from my going out, I heard his voice calling me from inside, so I quickly went in. Then he said to me, "Come, so I may pray for you." I knelt before him and he put his hand on my head and prayed a long prayer. Then he lifted his eyes to heaven and said audibly three times, "Forgive me, Lord Jesus Christ, I didn't know him."

I, then, left his place and went back [to my town] after I had taken a huge blessing from that visit. Two weeks had not passed on this visit before I learned of his passing away. I thanked my God for permitting me to take the blessing of, and seeing, Fr. Abdel Messih before his departure.

Father Abdel Messih the Ethiopian

Fr. Abdel Messih the Ethiopian was one of the Ethiopian monks who traveled from Ethiopia to Scetis on foot. He lived in a cave near the Baramos monastery, living as a solitary in fierce asceticism.

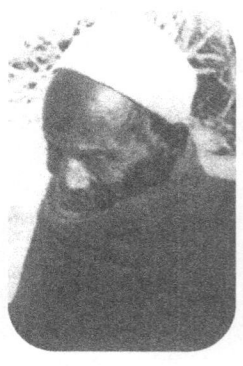

Some young men, who were lovers of the monastic [way of] life, used to come to his cave. One of these was Dr. Wadih Ameen. He was accustomed, when he visited the monastery of the Syrians, to pass by the cave of Fr. Abdel Messih the Ethiopian, to take his blessing and ask for his prayer, and to see with his own eyes a living example of a true monk, receiving from him a powerful impetus to help and encourage him to fulfill his own monastic longings to which he was looking forward.

Fr. Pimen relates to us some of his memories of Fr. Abdel Messih the Ethiopian when he used to visit him in his cave. His reverence says:

> Numerous times I visited Fr. Abdel Messih the Ethiopian the Solitary. During one of these visits, I went from the monastery of the Syrians to the cave of Fr. Abdel Messih the Ethiopian, and with me was a group of young men from the retreat house. We spent the whole day with him until sunset. He said to us, "Where are you going?" We said that we were going back to the retreat house in the monastery of the Syrians. He pointed with his hand to the direction we ought to take to reach the monastery. Then he blessed us and we left walking according to the direction he had pointed us to with his hand.

As we walked, we felt a spiritual power was guarding us and protecting us from the dangers we could have met on our way, especially as we were walking at night in the mountain. We felt also that a power was guiding and directing us to walk in the way he had pointed to us, so that we did not deviate to the right nor to the left. After walking for a short while, we found ourselves in front of the retreat house of the monastery of the Syrians. We thanked God for caring for us and protecting us throughout the way until we arrived safely.

Bishop Theophilus and the Monks of the Monastery of the Syrians

When Hegumen Theophilus of the Syrians was ordained bishop over the monastery of the Syrians with the name Bishop Theophilus, he opened the doors of the monastery to university graduates and Sunday School servants, and His Grace is considered the first to embrace university graduates and Sunday School servants. Therefore, a large number of these intellectuals thronged the monastery of the Syrians. One of these intellectuals and Sunday School servants was Dr. Wadih Ameen who had frequented the monastery of the Syrians since 1955 and received a bounteous amount of love of which Bishop Theophilus drenched people like him of the intellectual Sunday School servants. As Dr. Wadih's visits to the monastery of the Syrians grew in number, his relationship with Bishop Theophilus [likewise] grew stronger. All the monks, contemporaries of Fr. Pimen, testified of the love, respect and appreciation which Bishop Theophilus harbored for Dr. Wadih. This appreciation, respect, and love continued, and grew even stronger, after Dr. Wadih joined the monastery of the Syrians and became one of his children the monks. Owing to the frequent visits of Dr. Wadih to the monastery of the Syrians, a strong relationship was formed with the monks of the monastery, especially his fellows with whom he served in Sunday School, and others as we have previously mentioned.

His Relationship with The Departed Saints

Our Coptic Orthodox Church believes in the relationship between the heavenly and the earthly, that is, between the striving[110] Church on earth and the victorious Church in heaven. This relationship will continue until the Lord comes upon the clouds in His second coming, when the dead will rise in Christ, and we who are remaining, the living, will be all caught up together with them in the clouds to meet the Lord in the air; and so shall we ever be with the Lord.[111]

From this standpoint, we the believers will continue asking for the intercessions of the saints, supplicatory intercessions, offering them venerations and beatifications on account of their struggle and their triumph. Continually, each of us may take for himself an intercessor or more in particular, harboring for him love and homage, in admiration of his life and struggle, that he may become for us an intercessor in all our life's affairs.

Fr. Pimen was one of these who had a strong loving relationship with the heavenly, the martyrs and saints, first among them, the Mother of God, the pure Virgin,

---

110 Also: combatant.
111 1 Thessalonians 4:14–17.

St. Mary. From a young age, he loved reading their stories until his heart was kindled with their love, and they became to him an incentive and a good role model in the path of his striving.

Though Fr. Pimen had a relationship with many of the martyrs and saints, bearing love for them in his heart, his love and relationship with the Lady, Virgin Mary surpassed every love and every relationship he had. This was noted by these close to him when he talked about the Lady, Virgin Mary, and also when participated with his children the monks in the Praises service in the Kiahk vigils and the vigils of the feasts of Virgin Mary; you would see him in a state of passion, jubilation and spiritual joy.

Let us, dear reader, show you what we were able to see with our eyes and to pick out of his mouth when conversing about the heavenly.

The Virgin Saint Mary

> *"Your glory O Mary is higher than heaven, you are more honored than the earth and its inhabitants.*
>
> *"Therefore everyone magnifies you, O my Lady the Mother of God, the ever-holy.*
>
> *"And we also pray that we may win mercy, through your intercessions with the Lover of Mankind."*[112]

Fr. Pimen related to us the following of his relationship with the Lady, Virgin Mary. His reverence says:

---

112 Sunday Theotokia.

> I was accustomed to attending all the vigils which the monastery held in the feasts of Virgin Mary. It happened that during the vigil of the feast of the Assumption of the Body of the Lady, Virgin Mary on the 16th Mesore[113], while we were all in the Church of the Virgin of the Syrians, I saw the Virgin Lady appearing above us inside the Church. As she walked, she seemed joyful in the fathers the monks and their praising.

In this vigil specifically, all the monks felt a beautiful spirit different from other past vigils.

> After I saw this appearance of the Lady the Virgin, I told none of my bothers the monks of what I saw. I completed the praises with them, then attended Liturgy, and when finished, I went back to my cell to rest a little. When I woke up, I went out of my cell to fulfill some of my personal matters and to follow up the condition of the patients in the monastery. I noticed that every monk meeting me would say to me, "Father, why is your face shining like this?" I would deny this, but when their words were repeated to me many times, I said to myself, "Better that I sit in my cell, to avoid rumors." I preferred that I tell no one about seeing the Lady the Virgin and her being the reason behind my face shining.

There is another story showing Fr. Pimen's relationship with the Lady the Virgin.

An elderly lady came to the monastery of the Syrians on the 4th of August, 2007, and she was carrying a complete altar handkerchiefs set and a new oblation plate. She requested to meet Fr. Pimen and gave him

---

113 22nd of August.

the altar handkerchiefs and oblation plate, saying, "The sister who embroidered the altar handkerchiefs was not intending on sending them to your reverence, but the Lady, Virgin Mary appeared to her and told her that the altar handkerchiefs and the oblation plate ought to necessarily be sent to Fr. Pimen. But the sister to whom the Lady, Virgin Mary appeared, did not know your reverence, and when she asked me about your reverence, I told her that I knew you very well, so she gave me the altar handkerchiefs and the oblation plate, and asked me to bring them to your reverence. This is all what happened." Fr. Pimen took from the lady the oblation plate and altar handkerchiefs, thanked her, prayed that she may be blessed, and dismissed her in peace.

After hearing this story, many questions come to our mind. We may be able to answer some of them, but others are puzzling regarding their answer. Nevertheless, undoubtedly, all that happened confirms the existence of a strong relationship between the Lady, Virgin Mary and Fr. Pimen.

His reverence Fr. Pimen also spoke to us about his relationship with the Lady the Virgin, saying:

> One of the times I was returning from Qalyub to the monastery, and while I was driving my car at the beginning of the street in the public road, I saw a woman coming towards me. At the mere sight of her, something in me stopped me. The way she looked was very wondrous, inspiring her age to be that of an older woman of about 55 or 60 years of age. Her countenance, nevertheless, seemed to show strength and [good] health. She was wearing a long pale gray gown, and her head was covered with a scarf on top of which was a cloth headdress like a crown, likened to what

women wear in Upper Egypt. She approached the car window and stopped without saying a word to me. I thought she was a poor woman asking for alms, so I put my hand in the pocket of my cassock and I found a quarter pound bill, so I gave it to her. It seemed [to me] that she didn't like it, and she said to me, "Okay, half a pound[114] of meat." I found her answer strange. I mean [it is strange that] a poor person objects when you give him something like this. I give a little, somebody else gives a little, and she can get the meat she wants. However, it seemed to me that she was giving me a different lesson, not merely this story of half a pound of meat.

After that, she left me and went away, and I continued on my way to the monastery. I had feelings, however, that were unusual, because of what she said to me. I was feeling an exceedingly great consolation and had strange feelings that I had known this woman before.

When I arrived at the monastery and went into my cell, my eyes fell on a picture that was hanging of the Virgin Lady, and I continued staring at the picture of the Virgin the Queen; she was exactly the woman I met: the same look, the same details, the same everything. I wish I had gotten out of the car and made a prostration to her. How I spoke to her while sitting, and she standing! What gave me consolation however is that she took the money and did not refuse it.

He related this story while tears were pouring from his eyes, and he reproached himself severely because he did not know her. This was one of the many times

---

114 Literally: a quarter Kilo.

wherein the Virgin Lady appeared to Fr. Pimen as he mentioned in some of his conversations with his close children.

With the Anchorites

Fr. Pimen spoke to us about his relationship with the anchorites and his reverence said:

> It happened one day, [when] I was responsible for the retreat house, that I was sitting with two monks from the monastery in front of the house after Vespers. There weren't buildings or trees or anything blocking the view of the ancient monastery.
>
> Suddenly, we saw a small luminous cloud appearing in the sky and moving slowly towards the monastery. It then entered the ancient monastery. A little later another cloud, like the first, appeared and entered the ancient monastery also. This sight was repeated several times, that one of the fathers sitting [with us] was alarmed by the sight, but I said to him, "Calm down, these are the anchorites who have come to pray a Liturgy in the monastery."
>
> Also, on one of the Saturdays, I left my cell to go to the gathering for baking [bread], and Fr. Paphnotius of the Syrians (H.G. Abba Mettaos, bishop and abbot of the monastery of the Syrians) was walking with me. As we passed by the Church of the Forty Martyrs of Sebaste, we heard the sound of Liturgy coming from the Church, knowing that Liturgies are not prayed in the monastery on Saturdays. Fr. Paphnotius continued his way to the gathering, but I was curious to see the source of this marvelous sound.

Therefore, I went to the Church of the Forty Martyrs and opened the door of the Church. I saw the veil of the sanctuary withdrawn and the altar covered with altar handkerchiefs [for Liturgy], but I saw no one. So I realized that there were anchorite fathers who have come to pray Liturgy in the Church of the Forty Martyrs.

Besides this, we have mentioned previously that Fr. Pimen had a relationship with the saints before monasticism, such as the appearance of the Lady the Virgin to him at his sister's house, the appearance of Pope Kyrillos VI to him when he was going to the monastery, the appearance of Fr. Abdel Messih of Manahra to him in the clinic before he went to the monastery, and the appearance of two elders in his house before he went to the monastery.

All this indicates [the existence of] a firm relationship between Fr. Pimen and the saints. It also indicates Fr. Pimen's purity of heart which qualified him to see the Lady the Virgin, the anchorites and the saints. For the Gospel says, "Blessed are the pure in heart, for they shall see God."[115]

---

115 Matthew 5:8.

PART ONE

Father Pimen's Life

CHAPTER FIVE

Occurrences and Wonders

Occurrences and Wonders

"Come, see a Man who told me all things that I ever did."[116]

In the Psalm, David the Prophet describes the children of God who are meditating on His law, day and night: "He shall be like a tree planted by the rivers of water, that brings forth its fruit in its season, whose leaf also shall not wither; and whatever he does shall prosper."[117]

And in another place he says about these: "Those who are planted in the house of the Lord shall flourish in the courts of our God. They shall still bear fruit in old age; they shall be fresh and flourishing, to declare that the Lord is upright."[118]

The gifts that God gives His children are the fruit of their struggle, their patience through temptations and warfare of demons, and their purity of heart, with the work of grace in them. Some of the most prominent gifts God gave Fr. Pimen in his life on earth were his affectionate fatherhood and his wisdom, and his gifts in preaching, teaching, meditation, and exegesis of the word of God. Our beloved Fr. Pimen, however, had many occurrences and incidents, but even wonders, with those who had close interactions with him, measuring up to the borderline of miracles and were distinguished by clairvoyance. We rather present them to you, dear reader, as occurrences and wonders, letting you be the judge of them as you will. These, in any case, will neither add nor take away anything from Fr. Pimen, but at the same time they uncover to us the ripe fruits that came out of this tree, beside the virtues which his life testified of.

---

116 John 4:29.
117 Psalms 1:3.
118 Psalms 92:13–15.

There are many occurrences and incidents, jostling together in our mind. We will record a few of them, what is suitable to be recorded, that you may see in them the work of God's Holy Spirit and His grace through the person of our beloved Fr. Pimen.

The Locked Car Door

During one of the times wherein Fr. Pimen went out to Qalyub to bring some supplies and necessary medications for the monastery, he went to a pharmacy, parked the car in front of it, got out of it and locked all its doors. After walking a few steps, he immediately realized that the car keys were not in his hand and that he had forgotten them inside the car. When the pharmacist and the workers saw from afar Fr. Pimen perplexed, they came out and asked him about the reason. He told them that he had forgotten the car keys inside [the car] and had locked its doors.

A number of pharmacy workers gathered around the car and they all tried to open its doors but to no avail. One of these standing told them that he was going to get a specialist to open the door of the car. In a few moments all who were around the car went back each to their work until the arrival of the specialist. Meanwhile, Fr. Pimen remained standing beside the car alone, and raised his heart in a fervent prayer to God. One of the pharmacy workers noticed this from afar. A little later, Fr. Pimen walked toward the door of the car and extended his hand to the door handle. The door was opened immediately without any hindrances. When the worker saw what had taken place from afar, he hurried toward Fr. Pimen, along with the others who had previously tried to open the door, all running after him to look at this miracle which had taken place, all the while giving praise to God.

Knowing That He Is Sick

A trip was organized by one of the churches to [visit] the Natron Valley[119]. The bus went first to St. George's Monastery in Khatatbah, and there, one of the young men on the trip suffered from a severe stomach pain. When they finished their visit at St. George's Monastery in Khatatbah, they proceeded toward the monastery of the Syrians, then to the cell of Fr. Pimen, because the trip was a group of [church] servants. When they arrived at his cell, the young men got out of the bus and everyone greeted Fr. Pimen as they were getting out.

When it was the turn of the young man who was ill, Fr. Pimen asked him about his health, saying to him, "May God grant you speedy recovery." He quickly went into his cell and brought out for him medication which was for his stomach illness, without anyone telling him about the patient's condition or the type of his illness. When the members of the trip therefore saw what Fr. Pimen did, they marveled at his spirituality and clairvoyance. After that, he took them, sat with them on the ground outside his cell, and spoke to them, preaching to them the words of grace coming out of his mouth.

Stitching Without Surgery

One of the fathers the monks related [the following story], saying:

> Many years prior to my entering the monastery, we used to come to the monastery for visits, me

---

119 Scetis.

and my family. The late Hegumen Pimen would come and sit with us welcoming the family, because we had an old relationship with him before his tonsuring. During one of the times, my little sister, who was about 10 years old, had a small tumor under her chin. When Fr. Pimen saw her, he asked her about the tumor, so my mother said, "This is a tumor, father. I wish you would pray for her because they say a surgery is needed."

Fr. Pimen then put his hand on the tumor and began feeling it as though he were giving her an examination because he is a doctor also. He said to my mother, "Don't be afraid, no surgery or anything. There is nothing, there is nothing."

After we spent the day at the monastery, we went back home, and we found that the tumor had disappeared. We only found a trace of a small line like that of surgical stitching. We, then, knew that the hand of the Lord was stretched out with Fr. Pimen's hand and simply performed the surgery. We marveled, saying, "Marvelous is God in His saints."

He Knows About the Fire

There was a gas leak in the house of Fr. Pimen's sister, which caused fire to ignite from the stove. This resulted in some burns to his sister's face.

After the fire was put out, her husband quickly took her to the hospital, without telling anyone in the house, not even her mother who was staying with them in the house, in order not to cause any disturbance or anxiety.

In the hospital, the necessary aids were performed

on the patient, and medications were prescribed. She returned without delay to her house with her husband. The moment she entered the house, she received a phone call from Fr. Pimen, who was checking on her about the burns she had suffered. In amazement and wonderment, she put him at ease. She asked him about how he had known of what had happened even though no one knew of the ones staying in the same house with her. He did not answer her inquiries, but said to her, "You should thank God that your eyes were not harmed."

There lies before us a question, for which we have not known an answer. That is, how did Fr. Pimen know of what had happened to his sister?

Surprising One of His Children with the Results

In the third year of university was a student who was one of the [spiritual] children of Fr. Pimen. Due to the difficulty of the exams that year, he was troubled and was very worried about the results. He had asked Fr. Pimen to pray always for him, that the year would pass in peace and that he may pass his exams. Fr. Pimen used to always reassure and encourage him.

On the appointed day when the results were to be released, the student went to university where the results were attached to announce the names of the students who have passed and their rating. There he found that he had passed with "good" rating, so that he was very glad and he then went on his way. A few moments after he had learned of his good results, and before leaving the university, he was surprised by Fr. Pimen calling him and congratulating him for his success. Here the student remained silent for [few] moments, marveling at Fr. Pimen's knowledge of the results. He asked him about how he had known of the results, though only few minutes had passed since their release. Fr. Pimen digressed in his conversation with him, saying, "Didn't you get 'good?' Congratulations!" This made the student marvel even more after Fr. Pimen told him also the rating which he had received. The student thanked him and asked him to pray always for him. The question, however, remains unanswered: How did Fr. Pimen know the results, but even the rating which the student had received?

The Transfer Is Done by a Ruling of Removal

Fr. Pimen's niece used to work as a doctor in one of the health units in Alexandria. She encountered many problems from the management of the unit. She was even forced to lower her work hours by a third, to avoid the vexations she encountered at work. Even with all this, problems persisted. In her attempt to find any solution for herself, she submitted more than once a request to be transferred to another unit, but all her submitted requests were met with refusal, for a lack of someone replacing her.

When she could no longer endure the problems, she went to the monastery of the Syrians and met Fr. Pimen. She told him about her problems and what she suffered of vexations at work. Fr. Pimen reassured her and affirmed that her problem would be resolved, and that she only ought to buy a bottle of perfume and take it to St. Mina monastery, put half of it on the relics of St. Mina the Martyr and the other half on the relics of Pope Kyrillos. When she does that, the problem would be resolved for good.

His niece left Fr. Pimen and went back to her house. In the same week, she bought a bottle [of perfume], went to St. Mina monastery, and did as Fr. Pimen advised her. She had faith and trusted that her problem would be resolved.

A few days after her return from St. Mina monastery, the utterly unexpected happened. The governor of Alexandria passed by the health unit where Fr. Pimen's niece worked, and when he asked about the authorization [papers] for constructing the unit, he learned that it was constructed without authorization. He issued an order of removing the unit within 48 hours. Due to this ruling, the Board of Health Affairs was forced to distribute all the doctors who worked in this unit to other branches, and subsequently this distribution included Fr. Pimen's niece. She was transferred to a place much better than she had hoped for.

This is how through the prayers and guidance of Fr. Pimen, his niece was transferred and her problem resolved.

Offering Condolences Before Passing Away

Hegumen Pimen's nephew called on the day of the Feast of Nativity in 2007 to wish Fr. Pimen happy Feast, as he was accustomed to doing for the Feast. This time when he was wishing him happy Feast, Fr. Pimen answered him, saying, "May God be with you. Be strong. May the Virgin stand by you. The saints won't leave you..." His nephew marveled at Fr. Pimen's manner of speech with him and tried to inquire from him about the reason for which he said these words. However, Fr. Pimen did not disclose to him the reason.

Fr. Pimen's nephew gave the phone to his wife that she may also wish Fr. Pimen happy Feast, but what is strange is that Fr. Pimen answered her with the same words he had said to her husband, and even added to it more words of condolences as though he was consoling her. The call ended but Fr. Pimen's nephew and his wife were perplexed and surprised by Fr. Pimen's answers to them. Even the monk who was with Fr. Pimen, standing [near him] during the call and hearing Fr. Pimen's conversation with his nephew and wife, asked him about the reason for saying these words to them on the Feast day. Fr. Pimen answered him with general unconvincing words. The monk who was entrusted with serving him, asked him no more.

A few days passed on this call, and precisely on the Feast of Theophany, that the father of Fr. Pimen's nephew's wife passed away suddenly, with no complaint or illness. Three days later, her uncle passed away also. Here the mystery was revealed of Fr. Pimen's conversation with his nephew and wife on the Feast of Nativity, in that he meant by his conversation to comfort them and strengthen them prior to what was about to happen in the upcoming days.

Before this occurrence, we abstain from speaking, for we have no answer to this, except that we may say that these are spiritual matters of purity of heart and clairvoyance, which are beyond our understanding and are more exalted than that we may probe their depths.

Seeing His Guardian Angel with Him

One of the fathers the monks spoke of an occurrence that happened with him, saying that his brother in the flesh was suffering from cancer. Whenever he came to visit the monastery and his brother, they would go to take Fr. Pimen's blessing, that he may pray for him and anoint him with oil.

During one of these visits, whenever the brother who was sick stood to take Fr. Pimen's blessing that he may excuse himself to leave, Fr. Pimen would prevent him and say to him, "Stay a bit [longer.] Where are you going?" And he would insist on him staying. This was repeated several times.

After a while, the brother who was sick insisted on leaving, that he may rest and take his analgesic medications. Fr. Pimen in the end let him go. The monk, who is the sick man's brother, asked him to pray for him and anoint him, as he usually did every time, but Fr. Pimen refrained and said, "I can't pray for him or anoint him."

They were surprised by this answer and left perplexed. Later, the monk inquired about that. Fr. Pimen said to him, "How can I pray for him while his angel was standing beside him." No more than two days passed before his brother passed away to heaven. Here, the monk remembered Fr. Pimen's words about the angel standing by him, that is, his guardian angel. He marveled at Fr. Pimen's clairvoyance and his foresight.

PART ONE

Father Pimen's Life

CHAPTER SIX

His Last Illness and Departure

His Last Illness and Departure

"For I am already being poured out as a drink offering, and the time of my departure is at hand. I have fought the good fight, I have finished the race, I have kept the faith. Finally, there is laid up for me the crown of righteousness, which the Lord, the righteous Judge, will give to me on that Day, and not to me only but also to all who have loved His appearing."[120]

A Christian View of Illness and Death

Before Christianity, people's view of illness was that of a curse or the wrath of God upon man. However, after the coming of the Lord Christ, illness became a gift and fellowship of the sufferings of the Lord Christ. As the Scripture says: "For to you it has been granted on behalf of Christ, not only to believe in Him, but also to suffer for His sake."[121] The sufferings of illness, therefore, wherein the person who is ill shares the suffering Christ, count him worthy of heavenly glories with the risen Christ. As the Scripture says: "If indeed we suffer with Him, that we may also be glorified together. For I consider that the sufferings of this present time are not worthy to be compared with the glory which shall be revealed in us."[122]

Likewise, people's view of death before Christianity was that of horror, fear, and ceasing to exist. But after the coming of Christ, death became the golden bridge for crossing to the heavenly glories and immortality. As the apostle said: "For to me, to live is Christ, and to

---

120 2 Timothy 4:6–8
121 Philippians 1:29.
122 Romans 8:17–18.

die is gain."[123] For by the death of the Lord Christ, we triumphed over death; it became possible for us to enter the glories of the Resurrection with Him. For the Lord Christ defied death by his death, and so do we also, after we were united with Him in the likeness of His death (in Baptism), cry out in the face of death which desires to lay hold of us at the time of our death, saying, "O Death, where is your sting? O Hades, where is your victory?"[124]

Therefore, the holy fathers rejoiced in illness, and they desired death also, esteeming these to be things that would qualify them for the glory with the Lord Christ.

His Illnesses in His Last Years

"For as the sufferings of Christ abound in us, so
our consolation also abounds through Christ."[125]

The health of our beloved father Fr. Pimen began to deteriorate, and signs of old age appeared on him in the last years of his life. When the Lord desired to add to the glory of Fr. Pimen's crown, and to set in it a precious jewel that is the endurance of illness, the Lord allowed him to pass through numerous and very painful illnesses before his departure, as a prelude to leaving this world of misery; and also as a prelude for his children and his brethren in the monastery's community and all his beloved who knew him closely and dealt with him and enjoyed the blessing of his prayer—that they may prepare themselves for his departure from them.

Here, we, dear reader, are trying to survey for you the most important illnesses from which our beloved

---

123 Philippians 1:21.
124 1 Corinthians 15:55.
125 2 Corinthians 1:5.

Fr. Pimen suffered in the ten years before his departure. They affected his health, and he endured them patiently and with thanksgiving, considering them jewels with which God is adorning his crown.

Our beloved father suffered from pain in his vertebral column for a long time, lasting for about five years, starting from 2001 to 2006. When its negative consequences became worse and when its effect showed in his walking and his general movement, the doctors saw that performing a surgical operation was unavoidable. Our beloved father submitted to the counsel of the doctors who were treating him, and a very delicate operation was performed on him, to enlarge the spinal cord canal. This was done in 2006 when he was about 77 years old. The operation was successful, in that it stopped [further] deterioration of the condition of the vertebral column, but did not improve the consequences caused by the vertebral column's [condition] from difficulty of walking and whatnot. However, after the operation, Fr. Pimen was in permanent need for a cane in his hand beside the help of a person to support him when walking for very short distances. This condition accompanied him to the end of his life.

In 2005, Fr. Pimen suffered from prostate hypertrophy, which caused him severe pain. When the pains were intensified, surgical intervention became unavoidable. He submitted to the will of God, and an operation was performed on him to remove the prostate. A short while after, another operation was performed to complete the first operation. In 2009, two operations were performed on his eyes, which had negative consequences on practicing his favorite hobby—that is, reading.

Hegumen Pimen had suffered from diabetes for a long time, and in the last years, his blood sugar was high without a clear reason. Noted was also his inability and his refusal to take food, which led to a state of general weakness in Fr. Pimen's health.

All these illnesses which caused him pain, our beloved father Hegumen Pimen accepted with perfect submission to the will of God and with marvelous thanksgiving, even though they prevented him from practicing his talents and his virtues which were dear to him. The pain in his vertebral column and the complications resulting from it, prevented him from walking in the wilderness and going out there for meditation and prayer, though he loved the wilderness ardently. Likewise, the injury to his eyes prevented him from practicing his favorite hobby—that is, reading. The general deterioration of his health and his need for attendants with him to serve him, deprived him of solitude and constant seclusion [in his cell] which he practiced before his illness.

Signs Before Departure

Our beloved Fr. Pimen knew that [the time of] his departure drew near though he did not declare it to anyone. Numerous occurrences however revealed to us that he had knowledge of [the time of] his departure.

In the last days before his departure, he cried a lot, and his tears poured down his eyes copiously, especially when he heard a hymn or veneration for one of the saints. When he heard the hymn Golgotha or a hymn for the Lady the Virgin, his tears flowed so much that the attending father was forced to stop the hymn, to stop Fr. Pimen from crying.

When the attending father asked him about the reason for these tears, Fr. Pimen answered, [saying], "When I see the glory of the saints and I think of their toil for Christ's sake, and how greatly they offered Him, and I look at myself, I who am unable to offer anything like them—I cry." On another occasion, another [father] asked him the same question, and he said to him, "When I hear the beautiful Church hymns, I imagine the beauty of heaven with its hymns and praises—I cannot hold my tears."

[Here is] another marvelous occurrence that also happened showing Fr. Pimen's knowledge of the time of his departure. Fr. Pimen brought a gift and gave it to one of the fathers in the monastery, months before the occasion. The father refrained from accepting it, hoping that Fr. Pimen would postpone [giving it] until the time of the occasion. Fr. Pimen, however, insisted on giving it to him, and he said to him, "If I don't give it to you now, I won't be able to give it to you again." The father accepted it from Fr. Pimen, thankfully. Indeed Fr. Pimen passed away before this occasion, as though he had known of the time of his departure.

A short while before the departure of Fr. Pimen, his reverence went out to the city of Qalyub to finish some of the monastery's affairs. While in Qalyub, unconventionally, he called many of the people he loved that they may come to him, and he said to them that he wanted to greet them, so all came to him. One of these was his older sister who lived abroad, who at the time was visiting Cairo. She apologized much to him for her inability to come to Qalyub, for health reasons; but he insisted that she comes. When she tried to apologize again about not coming, Fr. Pimen seeing that she was resolved about not coming, he said to her, "Perhaps we won't see each other again." When he said these words to her, she came to him, took his blessing and greeted him.

During this time which Fr. Pimen spent in Qalyub, emaciation and weakness began to show on him, and the amount of bile rose up in his body, even so that the color of his eyes and body were changed, and this was clear to all.

Going Out for the Last Time

After the farewell trip to his beloved, Fr. Pimen returned from Qalyub to his beloved cell in the monastery of the Syrians, as though he wanted to bid it farewell as well before his departure.

He came back to the monastery of the Syrians on Monday, 11th of October, 2010. The amount of bile was remarkably increasing in his body, to the extent that the fathers who came to greet him advised him to immediately go to the hospital for treatment.

After doing the necessary arrangements to transport Fr. Pimen to the hospital on the next day, whenever the fathers prompted him to go out of his cell to go to the hospital by car, he would say to them, "Why are you in hurry? I am going either way. Why don't you let me stay in my cell for a couple of days?" This was because of his fervent love for his cell, for he knew he was not coming back to it again.

After the fathers who were around him pressured him, he submitted to them, and when he got into the car, he began greeting them, one by one, and said to them, "Pray for me a lot, a lot. Pray that our Lord may help me." Some of the fathers began crying, for they all realized that it was the last time they would see Fr. Pimen.

Fr. Pimen arrived at Victoria hospital in Alexandria, and his condition was very critical. The necessary tests and radiation were done for him. The results revealed that there was an obstruction in the bile duct, which was due to a cancerous tumor in the beginning of the pancreas.

Things were going from bad to worse due to the general weakness and extreme decline in blood pressure, which compelled the doctors to admit him into the intense care unit. This was on the 17th of October, 2010. The doctors then saw that a stent in the bile duct was necessary to be installed. Therefore, an operation was performed with a scope to install this stent. Because of the extreme weakness of his immunity, he had an acute pulmonary inflammation, thereby worsening the condition.

On Friday, the 29th of October, 2010, the muscle of his heart stopped at exactly five in the morning. The doctors performed for him the necessary procedures until the muscle of his heart moved again. He went into a complete coma afterwards, and continued to be placed on an artificial breathing device. Fr. Pimen continued in the coma for eight days until his spirit ascended to heaven, carried by the angels and saints.

The Lord loved Fr. Pimen. He wanted him therefore to partake of the same sufferings which He tasted on the cross. This is what his children who were with him felt in the last days. For when our beloved father was on the bed of his illness and his two hands were lifted up on pillows from here and there, like a cross, he resembled his Master on the cross. When Fr. Pimen asked for water to drink, they would moisten a piece of cotton in water and place it on his lips, like his Master to whom they offered a sponge moistened in vinegar. Finally, God wanted that the departure of our beloved Fr. Pimen to be on the day of the crucifixion of his Master, on a Friday. These are undoubtedly proofs showing the joy of heaven in [receiving] the soul of our beloved father.

His Departure and His Burial

"Father, into Your hands I commit My spirit."[126]

On Friday, the 5th of November, 2010, at about 8:20 PM, the spirit of our beloved father Pimen departed, amidst the rejoicing of the hosts of angels and saints in a heavenly celebration, joyful and awesome, befitting reverend father Hegumen Pimen, to meet the ones from the world of the spirit whom his spirit loved, saw and accompanied here and there, but this time their meeting will be forever after the release from the prison of the body.

Of the marvelous things with which the Lord desired to honor Hegumen Pimen is that the day of his departure from the body—or say, his heavenly birthday, 5/11/2010—was the same exact day as that of his ordination a monk (5/11/1972), after he had spent 38 years carrying the cross, in asceticism, striving and purity, which qualified him to receive the crown of eternal life. It might also be a divine ordinance that the Fortieth-Day Liturgy of Hegumen Pimen's departure was on the feast of the departure of St. Pimen the confessor.

A marvelous thing also is what happened at the moment of the release of Fr. Pimen's spirit. Two brothers were coincidentally near Fr. Pimen's cell at this time, at night. While standing there, they saw a large white dove appearing in front of them suddenly. It circled round about the cell many times, then disappeared suddenly. This was at the time of the release of Fr. Pimen's spirit from the body. After the news reached them of his departure at the same time, they realized the [meaning of the] mystery of the appearance of the white dove.

The fathers who had accompanied him in the

---
126 Luke 23:46.

hospital rose up to prepare his body [for burial], shrouded him, dressed him in his own priestly garments and a phelonion[127], and they placed him in a casket.

At noon of Saturday, the 6th of November, 2010, a car carrying him was headed to the monastery of the Syrians, followed by many cars carrying a large number of Fr. Pimen's relatives and those who loved him. When the car arrived at the monastery, carrying the body of Fr. Pimen, the fathers raced to bear the pure body upon their shoulders[128] until they brought him into the church of the Virgin Lady of the Syrians. They placed the pure body in front of the main sanctuary, and the funeral prayer ceremony began, with the attendance of H.G. Abba Mettaos, bishop and abbot of the monastery of the Syrians; H.G. Abba Sarapamon, bishop and abbot of Abba Pishoy monastery, who was the father of confession of the late Fr. Pimen; H.G. Abba Isodoros, bishop and abbot of Baramos monastery; as well as the community of the monks of the monastery of the Syrians, a multitude of the fathers the monks of the surrounding monasteries, and a large number of Fr. Pimen's relatives and those who loved him, who had heard the news of his departure and were able to attend to take his blessing.

After the funeral prayer was completed, the fathers carried the pure body and brought it into the sanctuary where they went around the altar three times. They, then, went down to the nave of the church, where they went around three times also before going into the sanctuary and circling once again. They, then, left the church, heading toward the mausoleum, amidst the sorrowful tolls of the bells and the tears of those present, until they placed him in the Western mausoleum beside the

---

127 Arabic: *burnos*.
128 Literally: upon their necks.

late Hegumen Wessa of the Syrians.

After the mausoleum was closed and they prayed the concluding prayer, they all went away, yet their minds continued remembering his fragrant [manner of] life, his noble incidents, and his wholly dedicated service for them.

We, his children, the monks of the monastery of the Syrians, ask him to intercede for us so that God may help us as He helped him, that we may complete our striving and our exile in peace, and that He may accept us unto Him, and appoint for us a portion and an inheritance in the heavenly Kingdom, to Him be glory in His Church from now and forever. Amen.

Occurrences After His Departure

"My Father has been working until now, and I have been working."[129]

Our Coptic Orthodox Church believes that death is not the human being's end of life; rather, it is a passage to a better life. This gives those striving on earth a hope in Eternal Life and lack of fear of death. This motivates us also to ask for the intercessions of our departed fathers and brothers, for they are alive interceding for us before the throne of grace.

God willed to reveal the righteousness of our late father Fr. Pimen, who spent his life hiding his virtues and his holiness. God willed to reveal them after his departure so that they may be witnesses to his righteousness and holiness. We recount, dear reader, some occurrences which took place after the departure of our father Pimen.

---

129 John 5:17.

Answering a complaint immediately

Fr. Pimen used to care for the poor[130], directly and indirectly, meaning that he gave gifts to the poor himself, and he entrusted people he knew to distribute gifts to the poor. Of these he entrusted with distributing the gifts to the poor was a consecrated sister.

Shortly after Fr. Pimen's departure, it happened that a poor lady went to the aforementioned sister at her house, and she asked her for a refrigerator. So the sister went to her private room and looked at Fr. Pimen's photo hung in her room. She spoke to him in a complaint, saying, "If you'd been here, the lady's problem would have been resolved, and we would have bought her a fridge." After she finished speaking, a very strong fragrance of incense filled her room, which was smelled by all who were present. This was a sign that Fr. Pimen heard her request.

The sister, then, left her room and sat with the lady who had asked for a refrigerator, and while sitting together, Fr. Pimen's sister, who had arrived few days past from abroad, called the consecrated sister, though she did not personally know her nor had she a prior relationship with her. She told her that she wanted to continue helping[131] the poor for whom Fr. Pimen cared before his departure. She also told her that she was ready to send the monthly aids which Fr. Pimen used to send. The consecrated sister thanked her for her love. And before the lady left the sister's house, an arrangement was made to buy a refrigerator for her. Here the sister marveled at how immediately Fr. Pimen answered her plea. When those near heard of what had happen, they glorified God, and realized how greatly Fr. Pimen cared

---

130 Literally: the brethren of the Lord.
131 Literally: serving.

for the poor even after his departure to heaven.

The Three Licenses in the Street

One of Fr. Pimen's [spiritual] children recounted, saying, "I was on a family trip to Alexandria, and afterwards I headed towards the monastery of the Syrians, and [we were to go] to Cairo after. Near the gates of Alexandria, I discovered that I did not have any licenses on me—neither my driver's license, nor the license for the car, nor my wife's license. I was forced to go back to look for them, but with no avail. So I went to a police station and reported the loss so that I could travel. When I left the police station, I told Fr. Pimen reprovingly—this was after his departure—saying, 'How could you leave us like this in the street without doing anything! Take care of it, father,' with many more words like this and stern reproofs. We continued our trip, afterwards, heading to the monastery of the Syrians.

Before arriving at the monastery, I received a phone call from the family [we visited] in Alexandria informing me that somebody had found the three licenses in the street and had taken them to the police station and left them there. It was the same police station where we had made a report. One of the workers in the station had volunteered to bring them to the house after taking the address from the report.

On arriving to the monastery and praying in church, we headed to the mausoleum of the fathers the monks to thank Fr. Pimen for helping us and for supporting us in this miraculous way.

A Blessing and a Healing

Mr. Alfons Sami Mikhael, an owner of a large wood shop, [from] Bihtaim, Shobra El-Khaima.

One day it happened that he received a transport truck loaded with wood. The driver and his associate went out of the truck and began loosening the ropes binding the wood. During this, a large quantity of wood fell on the driver and his associate. The driver suffered a leg fracture. As for the associate, his injury was more critical. He suffered a fracture in his pelvis, a fracture in the second and third vertebrae, and a broken nose. The two were taken in an ambulance to the hospital and they were in a very bad state. A report of the incident and the condition of the driver and his associate was released by the doctor [in charge]. Mr. Alfons returned home in a lamentable emotional state, because of the difficulties he was going through at work, for he was close to declaring bankruptcy, and because of the incident in front of his shop and the driver's and his associate's injuries. When his wife saw him very sorrowful, she asked him about the reason, and when he told her everything, she suggested that he put on the cassock which they had taken from Fr. Pimen a while back, and God willing, the problems would be resolved through the prayers and blessing of the Virgin [St. Mary] and Fr. Pimen.

Mr. Alfons took his wife's advice and put on Fr. Pimen's cassock. When he put his hand in the pocket, he a five EGP bill. Though they had lent the cassock to many to wear for a blessing, no one had discovered this five EGP bill, but it was a sign from Fr. Pimen to Mr. Alfons, assuring him that he would never forget him in his prayers even after his departure, and that the problems would be resolved.

The next morning, Mr. Alfons left his house heading for the hospital to check on the driver and his associate, especially because the doctors had considered performing some surgical operations on them. When he arrived at the hospital, he was surprised to see them in perfect health, and they had no fractures at all, in contrast to the previous day's reports. No surgical operations had been done on them. They left the hospital together thanking God for His care. A short while later, the problems at work began to be resolved and the well-being to prevail, through the blessing of Fr. Pimen's cassock and the five EGP which he had left in the pocket for a blessing.

Healing from a Kidney Stone

Mrs. Afaf Sami Mikhael, Mr. Emad Nasri's wife who lives in Shobra El-Khaima, says, "My husband suffered a severe abdominal pain. The required tests and radiation, which were done, revealed the existence of a stone and some sand in the kidney. The doctor at St. Marina private clinic transferred my husband to Dr. Youssef Dawod, the surgery, urology and endoscopy consultant in St. Mark hospital. After a second examination was done for my husband, whose condition was very critical, the doctor decided that an immediate surgical operation was necessary. The steps were taken to this purpose: blood work and echocardiography were done. The ECG revealed that the condition was not reassuring and that the patient's state was unstable. Nevertheless, the doctor insisted on performing the surgical operation immediately. After long negotiations with the doctor to [convince him to] prescribe medications for my husband to take for two days, the doctor submitted to out wishes. He prescribed medications for us and we went back home. My husband's condition was very dire. After returning home, my sister-in-law called to ask about my husband's health, and when she learned of what had happened, she suggested that we get Fr. Pimen's cassock which they had, to take his blessing. Indeed, she sent Fr. Pimen's cassock, and after he put it on and slept in it for two whole nights, he felt a marvelous comfort which he had not felt before because he was suffering a severe pain as a consequence of the stone, besides the pain caused by urine retention.

On the morning of the third day, my husband went to the bathroom. The stone and some sand came out with the urine. My husband was completely healed from all the pain he suffered due to the stone and urine retention, without [needing] surgical operation. The pain has not returned again until now, through the prayers of the Lady, Virgin Mary and the blessing of Fr. Pimen.

May the prayers of Fr. Pimen be with us all. Amen.

PART TWO

Father Pimen's Teaching

CHAPTER ONE

His Monastic Principles

His Monastic Principles

Of the necessary and important things for a monk is to place for himself clear and specific monastic principles to follow from the first day he enters the monastery until the last day of his life. Through these principles, his life and his conduct are formed inside the monastery. They also give to his existence in the monastery a meaning and structure.

We could realize the extent of the effect of monastic principles on a monk's life from his conduct, seriousness and commitment in his monastic life. For the monk who does not walk according to the specific monastic principles which he had set[132] for himself, is like a feather in the windward, his life moving and proceeding according to psychological excitements, and the influence of others and of the community in which he lives. At one time his life goes to the right, and at another to the left, and his life, flailing from here to there, passes and comes to an end without him realizing anything except the bitter tragedy he lives. The monk however who passes his life according to specific monastic principles is capable, with ease, of setting for himself a clear and specific program for the way he is following in his monastic life, and he has all confidence that, with God's grace, he will reach the harbor in peace.

We have all noticed that Fr. Pimen lived his monastic life from the first day of his entrance into the monastery of the Syrians until the end of his life on earth, according to monastic principles which he had set to follow in his life, and through Christ's grace, he was able to follow them to the day of his departure.

Truly there are numerous principles in the life of Hegumen Pimen. We saw, however, that it is sufficient to

---
132 Literally: sketched.

highlight the most important three monastic principles which were obvious in his life.

Immovable Continuance in the Monastery[133]

Many of the fathers of monasticism explained in their writings and sayings the importance of the immovable continuance of a monk in a monastery, and of not going out to the world except for necessity. The fathers found no better analogy to [describe] the monk who often goes out to the world than that of a fish which, if it went out of the water, would die[134]. So is case with the monk, that when he leaves his monastery for the world, he becomes a target for the deadly arrows of the world.

They also likened the monk, who does not continually abide in his monastery, to a tree which, if it were repeatedly translocated from its place and planted in many places, would bear no fruit[135]. Likewise, a monk's instability in his monastery and his frequent movements in the world cause him to bring forth no spiritual fruits. As it is said in the Psalm, "Those who are planted in the house of the Lord shall flourish in the courts of our God."[136] Therefore, from the time Fr. Pimen entered the monastery of the Syrians to live as a monk, he put it in his heart not to leave it except for necessity, and this was so. For this [very] reason also, he ran away from Bishop Theophilus the abbot to avoid being ordained a priest, and this may become a snare and a cause for going out for service in the world. As we mentioned repeatedly in other places in this book, he turned down [the offer of]

---

133 Or: abiding continually; steadfastness.
134 See *Give Me a Word: The Alphabetical Sayings of the Desert Fathers*, Wortley J., trans. (Yonkers, NY: SVS Press, 2014), Antony 10.
135 See *The Anonymous Sayings of the Desert Fathers*, Wortley J., trans. (Cambridge, UK: Cambridge University Press, 2013), N.204.
136 Psalms 92:13.

going out for service and turned down the bishopric, so that he may not leave the monastery and go out to the world, even though service and the bishopric are holy and profitable works. His eagerness to carry out his monastic principles, and his personal enjoyment of the life of solitude and Divine fellowship in the wilderness, protected him and prevented him from accepting this, so long as it may be a reason for going out to the world and leaving the monastery.

The reader must not understand from this that these living in the world are as though all perishing or are defiled—God forbid!—Instead, they follow another way to salvation different from the monastic way. The monk who goes out to the world for an errand or who goes out to the field of service in the world will not escape at all from the poison of the world, its deadly arrows and its burdensome influences which try to stir the passions dwelling in him.

All these fears, and others, were the main deterrents standing as a barrier in front of Fr. Pimen against going out to the world. He knew well that a monk is like a fish which, if it went out of the water, would die. Likewise, if he went out of his monastery into the world, he would expose himself to death. Even if he did not die, he would keep then nothing but only a name and a form, with no depth or fragrance.

Fr. Pimen believed firmly in this monastic principle. Therefore, he constantly refused, firmly, the offers to serve in the world. This belief made him abide, immovably, in the monastery, and bring forth much fruit.

Fr. Pimen is one of the few who immovably abode in the monastery, whose foundations were not shaken by the luster of service and its glory. This was in spite of H.H. Pope Shenouda's personal knowledge of him, and [in spite of] His Holiness' need, during the early period after his enthronement on the See of St. Mark, of the type of servants who, like Fr. Pimen, were educated, that they may help him in the service which expanded to many places.

The immovable continuance of Fr. Pimen in the monastery and not going out for service in the world, undoubtedly betrayed a strong relationship and love between him and God, which was much stronger than can be loosened by anything even if such a thing seemed to be holy, such as service and the bishopric.

Remembrance of Death

Voluntary death to the world is one of the most important monastic principles, which must be obtained by the monk in his life. As the natural death is a starting point towards eternity, so is death to the world a starting point towards a heavenly life on the earth of the monastery. How beautiful is St. Paul's saying, "If then you were raised with Christ, seek those things which are above, where Christ is, sitting at the right hand of God. Set your mind on things above, not on things on the earth. For you died, and your life is hidden with Christ in God."[137]

A monk, then, is a person who lives the first resurrection with Christ, after his resurrection from the tomb of the world, fetid with sins and transgressions, and joins a monastery wherein he lives heavenly days on earth. In his resurrection, he takes off all that is worldly: his words, his thoughts, his looks. Even his appearance which he had in the world he takes off and puts on a cassock, cowl and a girdle.

---

137 Colossians 3:1–3.

Thus, the monk, who is able to live the resurrection within the monastery, possesses a new manner in everything, which is the manner of the sons of God, inhabitants of the new heaven, or otherwise said, the new earth, that is the monastery[138].

How beautiful is the saying of St. Isaac the Syrian, "A merchant fixes his eye upon dry land, and a monk upon the hour of his death."[139] This is what our beloved father, Fr. Pimen looked forward to from the first day of his entry into the monastery. This was not hidden away from the eyes of the monks and laity, for Fr. Pimen had hung on the western wall of the reception room of his solitary cell photos of departed fathers of the monastery, keeping it always before his eyes. And his favorite sitting place was on the side facing the photos of the departed fathers.

The sight of the photos in front of Fr. Pimen made him always remember death, and urged him to remember his departed fathers who were victors and who departed to the place of rest, in order to stir up his longings to join them.

Yes, not only did this express the loyalty and love which Fr. Pimen had in his heart for his departed fathers and brothers, but at the same time, it revealed a hidden desire within him: a desire to take off for the enduring world with the departed fathers. A true monk is he who desires the hour of death, and considers it the hour of his marriage and of his crowning with the luminous crowns of righteousness. This was Fr. Pimen's desire at every moment, and not only when he sat looking at the photos of the departed fathers, in the outer guest room

---

138 Literally: that is the earth of the monastery.
139 *The Ascetical Homilies of Saint Isaac the Syrian*. (Boston, MA: Holy Transfiguration Monastery, 2011), 366.

of his cell, but also when he was in his inner chamber[140], where he had hung a beautiful saying above his bed on which he slept. It is a saying by St. Isaac, which says, "This very night, perchance, you will be my tomb, O bed."[141] Thus, in every place in Fr. Pimen's cell, there was a photo or a saying urging him to remember death. Therefore, when the hour of departure came to him, he feared not, nor did he tremble at it, for at every moment he had it in mind and waited for it with joy.

Solitude and Constant Seclusion in the Cell

The fathers considered the cell a the source of life for a monk, and if he remained outside of it for long, he would die. As St. Anthony, the father of monks, said, "Just as fish die if they are on dry land for some time, so do monks who loiter outside their cells."[142]

In spite of the intense wars and temptations facing monks inside their cell from the enemy of good, the Lord who is in their midst, transforms these into indescribable consolations and blessings. The fathers likened the monk in his cell to the three youths in the furnace,[143] for death encompassing them from every side was transformed into cool dew by the Fourth who was found in the furnace in their midst. The cell, which is a monk's source of death because of the intense wars and the pointed arrows towards him from the enemy of good, is a source of life for him by Christ who is in its midst.

---

140 Arabic: *mahbasa*, the private inner room of a cell.
141 *The Ascetical Homilies of Saint Isaac the Syrian.* (Boston, MA: Holy Transfiguration Monastery, 2011), 458,.
142 *Give Me a Word: The Alphabetical Sayings of the Desert Fathers,* Wortley J., trans. (Yonkers, NY: SVS Press, 2014), Antony 10.
143 See *The Paradise of the Holy Fathers* 2, Budge A.W., trans. (London, UK: Chatto & Windus, 1907), 14.

Our beloved father, Fr. Pimen realized this concept well. Therefore, he was very diligent about not going out of his cell except for necessity. He used to stay in it for long periods, [his cell] being as his partner who knew his struggles and his love for God. It extended afterwards to constant seclusion for days, then weeks, and finally for the duration of the Great Fast and other fasts, during which he never left his cell, except when necessity called to leave for a very compelling matter, and this occurred rarely.

Fr. Pimen firmly believed that constant seclusion in the cell and solitude are of the fundamentals of monastic life and are of its very important principles. This is what made him bring forth fruit inside his cell, for through staying permanently in the cell and the constant seclusion in it, he practiced unceasing prayer, praising, reading, meditation, fasting, and other spiritual practices, which tightened the bonds of his love for God. Thus, it filled him spiritually and with Divine consolation, which lifted him above the feeling of needing what is outside of God, outside his cell.

God revealed the relationship of love that was between Him and Fr. Pimen inside his cell. When a young man tried to take a photo of our beloved father's cell, a wonderful photo of the face of Christ appeared which was shaped by the leaves of the trees planted around his cell, thereby announcing to us that God was with Fr. Pimen inside his cell and He chose it as His dwelling place.

I would like to draw the reader's attention to [the fact] that the distancing of Fr. Pimen from his brothers the monks and remaining in his cell for long periods, followed by constant seclusion for weeks, then for the fasting periods, was the result of one thing only, that is his love for God. For this [reason], he used to hang on the wall of his cell a saying by one of the fathers, which says, "Love all men, but keep distant from all men,"[144] and another saying, "Know that you are a monk and must not care about anything."

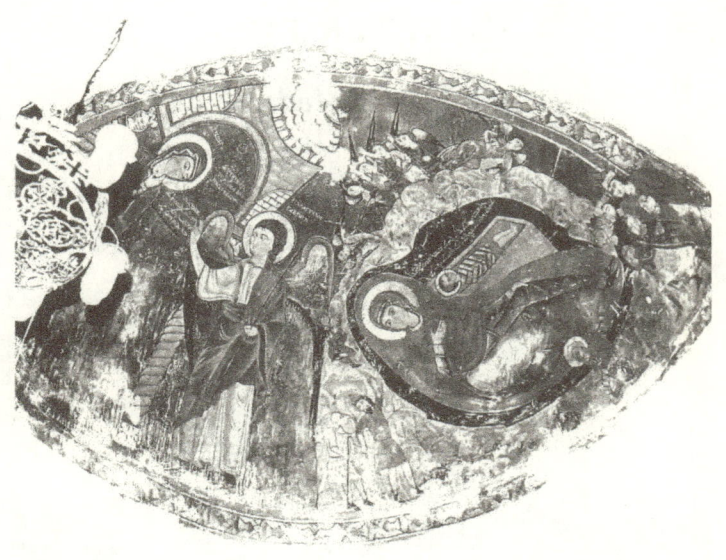

---

144 *The Ascetical Homilies of Saint Isaac the Syrian.* (Boston, MA: Holy Transfiguration Monastery, 2011), 457.

PART TWO

Father Pimen's Teaching

CHAPTER TWO

His Spiritual Meditations

On Repentance

The person who defends himself, pampers himself or cares about himself, is not repentant, because repentance is accompanied always by feelings opposite to these. It is accompanied by brokenness, humility, humiliation, feeling of unworthiness, grieving for himself, not lifting up his gaze, mourning for his sins.

Therefore, the great fathers always gave to monks the advice of, "Go into your cell and weep over your sins," because the cell is the place of weeping.

St. Isaac says, "There is a man who sits in the cell for a hundred years and [who] knows not what the sitting in the cell is, and there could be another man who sits in silence and calmness, like he who is in the prison of the repentant."[145]

Repentance is the exchange of love for love, exchanging the love of sins for the love of Christ. There are people who are sentimental, and there are others who are callous. The sentimental person may fall into [the sin of] uncleanness, but with the same degree and ardor, he is inflamed with love for God. Many of the adulterers are examples of this, who became great saints, having an inflamed sentiment which is full of love, and this love and this sentiment are directed towards God. But the hard-hearted person has to triumph over hardness of heart with reading and exercises, and ought to soften his heart and place in front of himself the example of St. Moses the Strong.

Repentance also delivers a person to humility, but he has to know that humility is a degree higher than a person [merely] judging himself. Humility needs great

---

[145] A similar saying a attributed to Abba Ammonas. See *Give Me a Word: The Alphabetical Sayings of the Desert Fathers*, Wortley J., trans. (Yonkers, NY: SVS Press, 2014), Poemen 95.

struggle, because it is a way of life. Just as repentance is not only temporary but is life, so is the monastic life a life of repentance, because it is a new life with God, in which a monk forgets his old life and reaches forth to those things that are ahead. But it is regrettable when a monk falls into new sins as if his sins from the world were not enough.

Repentance differs from one person to another, according to their sense of sin. Repentance begins first with the fear of God's punishment for sin, and by growing in spiritual life and the life of repentance, it becomes a repentance that is love of good and holiness, love for God in Himself, and remoteness from all that separate him from this Beloved.

Through repentance, a person enters into the degrees of purity, and it[146] walks him in the way of perfection. When he is walking in the way of perfection, he feels that he is weak and continually falls short, and that he needs God's help because he has not reached perfection yet. The life of repentance is an unending life, for we are under weakness and sin; therefore, we repent every day.

On Obedience

Obedience is, first, to God; second, to the rules of the monastery and its head; third, to any person within the limits of the commandments, and to all within the limits of the obedience of our Lord Jesus Christ.

Obedience requires the cutting off of personal desires, that is, the denying of the personal will, and as long as a person has his own will, he is not able to do

---

146 Repentance

the will of another. Obedience requires humility also, because with that humility, he sees that his opinion is wrong, and with humility, he can obey another's opinion and abandon his own. The obedient person, and he who cuts off his desires, has faith in God and in his elder, meaning that he trusts in him and performs his words, and God does not abandon him even if the guide errs.

Obedience is the disbelief in the self. The Lord Christ says, "If anyone desires to come after me, let him deny himself, and take up his cross, and follow me."[147] Here he says, "deny himself," that is to abandon it, and it no longer has any value. This feeling must be real and not feigned.

Of old, in the beginning of early monasticism, the simplicity of the disciple and his obedience, along with the holiness of the elder and his guidance which is supported by the Spirit of God, held the disciple's hand and brought him to high spiritual summits; for example, St. Theodore the disciple of Abba Pachomius the father of Koinonia, and his marvelous obedience to his elder; and the obedience of St. John the Short, also, to his elder, which left a great mark, that is, the tree of obedience. But in our era, there is negotiation, arguing and stubbornness with the [spiritual] guide; therefore, we do not benefit and do not reach the stature of any of the early fathers.

Obedience is dual faithfulness: from the confessor to the father of confession, and from the father of confession to the confessor.

As to the confessor: that he may favor the command of the father of confession over his own guidance and his opinions and his personal inclinations.

But as to the father of confession: his faithfulness

---
147   Matthew 16:24.

is to take hold of the confessor, to lead him in a sound path, and to correct him until he stands on his feet and until he does not blunder like a child, always in need of him; but he helps him to grow in grace until he becomes, himself, also a guide to others.

It is also possible to liken the way a father of confession deals with his son to a mother dealing with her little child. A mother does not always carry her son lest she causes him softness of bones, but she leaves him at times to learn how to walk, and when he falls, she quickly intervenes to deliver him. Likewise with the father of confession, he gives a chance for his son to learn the arts of spiritual life, how to walk in it, and learn the virtue of discernment, so that the son does not get confused if the father leaves him for any reason.

As a mother teaches her child to walk, so does a father of confession with his son, for he makes him walk step by step and does not make him leap onto high steps, because leaps are not profitable in monasticism but small steps that are achievable.

Here, we should say that a beginner's fervor[148] stands sometimes as an obstacle in the way of obedience, for example, [his desires for] abstinent fasting, the length of its duration, and also night vigil. It is as though the beginner wants to become [like] St. Anthony in two weeks after his entry into the monastery.

Many of the beginners tend to bodily virtue before the commandment, such as fasting, prostration, silence, constant seclusion [in the cell], and such virtues which are linked to the body, and they do not think of the spiritual virtues, which are more important, like love, long-suffering, patience, chastity, and the greatest one in monasticism, that is, purity of heart, through which

---

148 I.e. spiritual zeal.

he sees God in his heart.

Moreover, some of the mistakes confessors fall into:

✤ The concealment of certain sins, and not confessing them, whether because in their view they are shameful sins; or perhaps simple, trivial sins which should not be mentioned; or sins of thought, because he is not responsible for them, for they come and go, and he has nothing to do with them; and so on. This leads to difficulty in pulling them out from him, and getting rid of them. Consequently, their forgiveness relies on confessing them.

✤ Performing some exercises which he reads about, without [asking] the father of confession for his blessing, because if he asked his father of confession, he might say to him, "It is not [the right] time." An example of this is going out to live in caves or going out with the anchorites.

✤ His dependence on his own intelligence, though he may have no experience, especially in monastic life, as though spiritual life and walking with God depended on intellectual abilities. An example to follow is Abba Arsenius, who, in spite of his intelligence, his knowledge, and his mastering the Roman and Greek languages, would sit with the Egyptian elders asking them about his thoughts, saying, "I have not yet learned the alphabet of this rustic."[149]

For a period of time, confession was done publicly at church, as we read in the story of St. Moses the Strong, but the Church saw [that it is more favorable] that confession be done in a quiet sitting between the

---

149 *Give Me a Word: The Alphabetical Sayings of the Desert Fathers*, Wortley J., trans. (Yonkers, NY: SVS Press, 2014), Arsenius 6.

father of confession and his son, because of the negatives [associated with] public confession, which may cause others to stumble and cause the hearers to fall into pride, feeling that their sins are simple relative to some of the repugnant and difficult sins that are recited.

Finally, I would like to give an advice to monks: Obey the bell of the monastery, for it awakens the demons also, to fight the monks.[150]

On Meekness and Anger

The meek person is he who is calm, joyful, good-natured, amicable—that is, easy to deal with—is not obstinate, does not get angry, is not cruel, does not cling to his opinion; life with him is easy, a person whose company is easy and you do not get tired from dealing with him; he walks softly and in simplicity with everyone, and does not use violence.

[He is] a man who is simple, who does not know guile, malice, nor political schemes; a man minding his own, who does not argue and does not race for a position, a rank nor even for a word of thanks.

The meek is also humble, for meekness and humility are interconnected. The nerves of the meek are calm; his voice, calm; his countenance, calm. In dealings, he is as a light breeze passing by people, who does not jostle people in the path of life; therefore, he is always loved by people, "for the best of people [are these] who care not about the world in whosoever's hand it may be." But the person who inserts himself a lot in matters, and who

---

150 See Saint John Climacus, *The Ladder of Divine Ascent*. (Boston, MA: Holy Transfiguration Monastery, 2001), 127.

suffers and grapples—this person loses his meekness.

The meek, also, does not complain and is not restless, for he is a good man. The word "good" fits him in all its meanings. He does not reprove much but dismisses matters quickly, simply and calmly. Therefore, no one is afraid of the meek.

The Lord Christ said in the Beatitudes, "Blessed are the meek, for they shall inherit the earth,"[151] and the meaning of "they shall inherit the earth" is this: first, [they inherit] this earth we are living upon; that is, they inherit the love of people and good remembrance. Second, they inherit the earth of the living, that is, the heavenly Jerusalem.

There are people who are meek by nature, but if you are not one of these, listen to what the Lord Christ says to you, "Learn from Me, for I am gentle and lowly in heart, and you will find rest for your souls."[152] For meekness gives rest to the soul.

There are also people who love grandeur. These do not incline to meekness, and look to the meek with contempt and [see meekness] as weakness. In contrast with the meek, the angry person acts quickly and is a hasty person, and if he slows down, he may [be able to] amend his behavior. The meek person, on the other hand, takes matters slowly, does not answer hastily, for the word "meekness" in Greek carries the meaning of slowness and deliberateness. Therefore, St. Paul the Apostle says, "Give place to wrath;"[153] that is, give place through which it may leave and go away from you. St. Dorotheos says, "Do not resist evil, do not avenge yourself, do not be overcome by evil, but overcome evil

---

151 Matthew 5:5.
152 Matthew 11:29.
153 Romans 12:19.

with good[154], for the irascible man is overcome by evil."

The irascible man in anger repays with the same [measure]:

1. The first degree of repaying with the same measure is that you answer a word for a word, an action for an action, evil for evil.
2. You may not answer word for word but your countenance may show that you are perturbed, or that you may answer with a gesture or movement.
3. If you heard that something bad befell the person who had insulted you, you are pleased and rejoice, perhaps because God had avenged you, or because this happened to him in order that he may taste what he does to others.
4. If you hear that God dealt well with this person, who had insulted you, and you do not rejoice for him, then know that you have a heart that repays evil for evil, and does not rejoice for good. In this heart, God does not dwell.
5. If you did not pass through any of these stages and you forgave him, but when this person does a new mistake, you remember all his old [mistakes], this means that there is deposition[155] of anger, and though on the surface you are clear, at the occurrence of any new thing, you are stirred and remember all that had passed, and you erupt.

The opposite of this is the meek person, who always overcomes evil with good, inwardly and outwardly, because the meek, when they err against him, does not lose any of his love. The meek always blames himself

---

154 Romans 12:21.
155 That is, anger has settled below the surface and is hidden.

and walks in humility, and tries to turn away anger from others even if that leads to his loss, whether materially or morally, but in that he is sure that he is walking in the triumph of Christ, and with Christ this is far better.[156]

Here, I would like to say that a person is capable of distinguishing by his inward senses whether the word "I have sinned," which is said to him as an apology, is said with humility and sincerity, or not. If it were so, then it would persuade him to return, for a prostration is not [merely] the bending of the body and head down to the ground, but first, it is the contrition of the head and soul to the ground, as David the prophet says, "My soul clings to the dust."[157]

Here we mention an occurrence with Abba Pimen[158] when a brother asked him, saying, "Tell me, why when I do a prostration to a brother who is angry with me, I find that he is [still] dissatisfied with me?" The elder answered him, [saying,] "Tell me in truth, when you do a prostration to him, is it not in your mind that you are doing this, not because you have sinned against him, but only for the sake of the commandment?" The brother said, "The matter is so." Then, the elder said to him, "For this reason, God does not allow the brother to be satisfied with you, because you repent to him not of your will, but as if you had not sinned against him but that he was the one who had sinned against you."[159]

Good company teaches a lot. A man learns meekness from living with the meek, and humility from living with the humble. He who associates with the saints, imitates them, or feels that he is very small in front of

---

156 Philippians 1:23.
157 Psalms 119:25.
158 Also: Poemen.
159 Cf. *The Paradise of the Holy Fathers* 2, Budge A.W., trans. (London, UK: Chatto & Windus, 1907), 118.

them; thus, he obtains, for himself, humility.

There is a man who does not get angry [himself] but makes others angry, while remaining calm himself. Such a man has fallen into the sin of being a stumbling block. Therefore, if you anger another [man], try to calm him down, but know that there is a difference between two things: If you defend yourself to calm another [man] down, then this is a virtue; [but] if you defend yourself to justify yourself, this is a sin.

There is an irascible man who pours his anger into another's ears, thereby making the man angry along with him, and then a third [man] and so on. Therefore, do not cause others to stumble alongside you, and do not cause them to think evil of others of whom they thought well.

And here is a golden advice I say to you: Overcome the devil in the arena wherein he has overcome you.

On Mourning, the Mother of Joy

Joy that is born of mourning is divine joy. The joys of the world, however, become transformed into sorrow, of which the Lord Christ said to his disciples, "You will weep and lament, but the world will rejoice; and you will be sorrowful, but your sorrow will be turned into joy."[160]

This joy is the inner consolation which is felt by none except the man who is acquainted with repentance, contrition of heart, and mourning over his sins. Here, contrition of heart, repentance and regret,

---

160 John 16:20.

are transformed into inner consolation. Solomon the wise says, "For by a sad countenance the heart is made better;"[161] therefore, acquire sadness in your heart and do not show it before people. St. Arsenius used to continue in mourning and weeping, even until his eyelashes fell off, but with people he was joyful. People might be troubled by your frowning and might have thoughts of suspicion about you, or they might intervene to comfort you. Therefore, do not reveal yourself, nor your inner emotions, to anyone.

The righteous man chastens himself continually over every mistake he discovers, and does not flatter nor justify himself, but faithfully settles accounts with himself and corrects it with fasting, prostrations, rebuking and name-calling. A man may accept his self name-calling but may not accept it when others call him names. If a man angers him, he reproaches and blames himself, as Abba Amoun, the founder of monasticism in the region of Nitria, said, "The proper way and manner for a monk to live is to condemn himself continually."[162] And as St. Macarius the Great, the father of the wilderness [of Scetis], said, "My brother, judge yourself before they judge you."[163] From reproaching and judging oneself, sorrow is born within.

Because of these feelings which are born within, the man continues to live the life of continual repentance, and feels that he is a sinner, treats himself as a sinner, and accepts people's treatment of him as a sinner. Therefore, the feelings of humility continue always with him.

---

161 Ecclesiastes 7:3.
162 *The Paradise of the Holy Fathers* 2, Budge A.W., trans. (London, UK: Chatto & Windus, 1907),116.
163 Cf. *Give Me a Word: The Alphabetical Sayings of the Desert Fathers*, Wortley J., trans. (Yonkers, NY: SVS Press, 2014), Ammonas 10. Here the story is attributed to Abba Ammonas.

Humility, then, is not that you slander yourself vainly, but humility is that, if you were slandered from outside[164], you accept it with joy and contentment. An example of this is the story of Abba Serapion when a roaming brother came to him. Abba Serapion said to him: "Hitherto you were saying: 'I am a sinner' … and yet you became so angry when I lovingly admonished you? If you want to be humble, learn to tolerate courageously that which is said to you by others and do not apply meaningless words to yourself."[165]

These feelings, which are also called "a sense of reverence," are what St. Isaac calls "a reverntial posture" in which [one] appears before God. The reverntial man is not only loved and honored by people, but also by the angels surrounding him.

There are types of mourning:

1. **Mourning from [one's] nature**: that is, a man who has tender feelings and effusive sentiments, who cries for the simplest reasons.
2. **Mourning from afflictions**: this is because of the trials and tribulations which have befallen him.
3. **Mourning for sin**s: when a man thinks of his sins, their great number and ugliness, he weeps, and this leads him to repentance; but beware of despair.
4. **Mourning from remembrance of death**: this grants the person a perpetual readiness to meet death, and rids a person of many sins.
5. **Mourning out of divine love**: this is the most supreme type of them all. When a man thinks about

---

164 By others, that is outside of one's will.
165 *Give Me a Word: The Alphabetical Sayings of the Desert Fathers*, Wortley J., trans. (Yonkers, NY: SVS Press, 2014), Serapion 4.

God's love for him, what He has done for him, His forgiveness, His incarnation, His sufferings; what He has prepared for him in the Kingdom, the beauty of God and His glory; how God deals with him, him in particular—here the man stands incapable of expression, and finds nothing before him but weeping.

An important advice: Do not think about tears themselves but about their cause, which is sin.

On Remembrance of Death

The monk is a man who has died to the world. But, has he truly died? Is he behaving as a dead man? Or is the world still alive in him?

If when you hear an offensive word, and anger is stirred in you, or if you rejoice for a word of praise, are you in this case then dead? And if you still fear animals or beasts, or if you are afraid of walking in the mountain because of beasts and snakes, are you in this case dead then? Practicing death is a long topic.

Therefore, Paul the Apostle says, "So then death is working in us, but life in you."[166] The monk must first pursue the mortification of the senses of the flesh, for he prays every day and says, "Put to death our carnal lusts, O Christ, our God."[167]

The person who has truly died, by his will, does not afterwards fear the second death. The hour of death comes, and death finds nothing alive in him, and he hears the angels blessing him, saying, "Well done, good steward."[168]

The fear of death terrifies the heart of the foolish man; as for the saint, death is for him as life, but death is even more desirable than life, as the Apostle says, "To die is gain."[169]

The fear of death indicates lack of readiness for it, but he who has died to the world desires to be with Christ, "With Christ, which is far better."[170]

The devil makes a man hope for long life so that he

---

166 2 Corinthians 4:12.
167 Ninth Hour of Agpeya—Litanies.
168 Luke 19:17.
169 Philippians 1:21.
170 Philippians 1:23.

may gather for himself materialistic longings and worldly things in his heart, and he pursues their fulfillment because he will live a long life. Life and its luxury go hand in hand; as for the remembrance of death, it is consistent with, and goes along, asceticism.

Therefore, the Church placed the remembrance of death numerous times in the Prayers of the Hours (Agpeya), so that a person in general, and a monk especially, may place the remembrance of death before his eyes. For example, in the litanies of the Twelfth Hour, "Behold, I am about to stand before the just judge," and in the Veil prayer, "Lord, Your judgement is dreadful", and in the Midnight watches, "O my soul, consider that awesome day… with a compassionate eye consider my weakness, O Lord, for very soon my life will come to an end." Also in the Absolution of the Priests, "Help us to overcome the pangs of death, before death and after death."

Lord, make me to know my end, and what is the measure of my days, that I may know how frail I am. Indeed, You have made my days as handbreadths, and my age is as nothing before You[171], because the life of man is even a vapor that appears a little time and then vanishes away[172]. When the Master Christ—glory be to Him—spoke the parable of the unjust steward, He said at the end of the parable, "So the master commended the unjust steward because he had dealt shrewdly."[173] The master here is the master of that steward, and not the Master Christ; and he commended him, here, because he thought about his eternity and thought about the end of his stewardship over the goods of his master, whether they will receive him or not. Because he thought about

---

171 Seec Psalms 39:4–5.
172 See James 4:14.
173 Luke 16:8.

his eternity and prepared for it, his master commended him, that he had dealt shrewdly.

With this thought, that is, the thought of death, and preparation for it, many of the fathers walked and placed it in front of them, like St. Arsenius when he said, "Truly, the fear that is with me in this hour has been with me ever since I became a monk,"[174] and like Amma Sarah, who said, "When I put my foot on the ladder to go up, I also set death in front of my eyes before I go up there,"[175] and the saint who said, "I am afraid of three things: the moment when my soul is going to exit the body; the moment when I am going to meet God, and the moment when sentence is going to be given against me."[176]

The man who possesses the remembrance of death in himself, possesses nothing of this world's possessions, except what he takes along with him at the hour of death, that is, his works, for his works follow him[177]. He does not care about what he is not taking with him, and his manner of life proclaims, "Naked I came from my mother's womb, and naked shall I return there."[178]

There are people who do not like the mention of death and who run away from it; therefore, they are not prepared for it. Let us meditate on the stories of some of the saints, how their spirit departed from their body; and also in contrast, how the spirits of some of the sinners departed. The hour of death was restful to the saints, but to the others, terrifying. The saints sometimes see visions and revelations which gladden

---

174 *Give Me a Word: The Alphabetical Sayings of the Desert Fathers*, Wortley J., trans. (Yonkers, NY: SVS Press, 2014), Arsenius 40.
175 Ibid., Sarah 6.
176 Ibid., Elijah 1.
177 Revelations 14:13.
178 Job 1:21.

them, but the others, grievous sights, so they fear and tremble.

There are people whose [time of] death lasts for a considerable period of time until the spirit leaves the body which is accompanied by suffering; but others die peacefully. These are the judgements of God which are unsearchable.

For man will inevitably die, but the wise is he who dies by his own will. As for the foolish, he dies against his will. There are people whose mission does not end with their death, but [they] appear to people, and God sends them to complete tasks for the service of men. There are others who, after death, were gone and their names forgotten.

Let us take examples of this: God sends St. George to fulfill many works after death. St. Ignatius of Antioch in the same night after his death, appeared to encourage his brothers in prison. St. Paul the Apostle, used to appear to St. John Chrysostom, explaining to him his epistles. Abba Macarius the Great appeared, on the day of the consecration of the sanctuary after his name, and spoke to Pope Benjamin. All this is because they were worthy, that their message be extended on earth, even after their death.

Some people are a heavy burden on earth, and by their death, heaven and earth find rest. Others, the earth is saddened for their death, and heaven rejoices at receiving them, and they complete their message from there.

Death for the evil is an end of life, but for the righteous is a continual life.

There are people, whose bodies at the time of their death are very heavy, and are carried to the cemetery with difficulty. While others, you feel that their bodies are light, as if they are hastening on their way.

The bodies of some decompose; while the bodies of others remain sound, become a source of miracles and holy relics in churches, and people are blessed by them. Therefore, the Holy Scripture said on the mouth of Balaam the son of Peor, "Let me die the death of the righteous, and let my end be like his!"[179]

There are those whose spirit is carried by the angels to their eternal fate in joy, like what Abba Anthony saw at the time of the departure of Abba Paul [the First Hermit][180]. He saw angels carrying him with joy into heaven, for the angels carry the righteous in celebration like a bridegroom to his wedding.

And the evil [man] is encircled by demons at [the time of] his death, and is violently drawn away into hell. Are you able then to say about yourself like what the Lord Christ said, "For the ruler of this world is coming, and he has nothing in Me?"[181] If you had something in you belonging to the devil, fear, then, lest he asks for it at the hour of your death. Do not forget that one member defiles the whole body, for if your eye is bad, your whole body will be full of darkness.[182] And here St. Basil has a suitable saying: "What do I benefit if I worked all righteousness, and said to my brother, 'you fool,' and I shall be in danger of hell fire."

There are people also for whom the Lord Christ Himself came to receive their spirits, like the Virgin St. Mary and like Abba Karas the Anchorite. [Their] death was accompanied by sweet aromas and melodious heavenly hymns.

---

179 Numbers 23:10.
180 See *The Paradise of the Holy Fathers* 1, Budge A.W., trans. (London, UK: Chatto & Windus, 1907), 02.
181 John 14:30.
182 Matthew 6:23.

Finally, am I ready for sudden death and can I endure it? The teacher Mikhael El-Batanouny used to repeat a beautiful saying, and he would say, "Take me not, Lord, at the hour of oversight." We read in the biography of the martyrs that thirty thousand people from Damanhur walked to Alexandria, rejoicing at meeting death; and also the martyr who kissed the chains in which he was to be martyred.

There is an important truth: at the hour of death, a man is exposed as he is in truth, and he cannot hide himself.

On Meditation and Thanksgiving

Meditation is Adam's first order. With meditation, we abandon the things which made us lose our clairvoyance, which veiled from us the light and the connection and the full nourishment in Him.

Therefore, meditation gives us an opportunity to abandon, though for fleeting moments, disruptions and impurities, and gives us an honest, clear answer, to which we must cling, in a world of darkness and inconstancy.

The mind is the sound scale for everything, and often it judges with partiality toward the body and the heart and the general inclinations; therefore we see the various errors of the mind in science and philosophy. It is not so with the spirit, for it draws from the constant radiant source that does not change, where "every good gift and every perfect gift is from above, and comes down from the Father of lights, with whom there is no variation or shadow of turning."[183] This is God the Spirit.

---

183 James 1:17.

What is the difference between us and the great saints, like the great fathers of monasticism? For the desert is the [same] desert, the Holy Scriptures are the same, God is the same, His heaven is the same, mankind is the same. We, however, lack the burning heart[184], the strong spirit, the thirsty soul which is not assuaged except by frequenting the water fountains.

Meditation grants a view that is broad-ranged and farsighted. If I looked to myself, I would see before me my work, my future, my responsibilities, and my problems. If I am lifted up onto the rock of meditation, I see the whole world as a single unit. I find that people are born, toil, live in wickedness, then die, and I see myself as one of them, drowning in my problems, going through its toils and sufferings. In its inundations, the man might lose the true way leading him to the salvation of his soul and its eternal happiness. Without abandoning all these and without rising above them, we will not reach such a revelation nor the way.

In meditation, we may reach treasures, and these treasures are considered nothing unless they find their way into practical life and application.

Meditation is the practical application of faith, for it is "the substance of things hoped for, the evidence of things not seen."[185] Therefore, the Apostle said, "While we do not look at the things which are seen, but at the things which are not seen."[186] If it is not seen, how are we looking at it, unless this were through meditation, because that which is seen is earthly but that which is not seen is eternal[187]. Meditation, then, is the eye of the soul with which it sees.

---

184 Luke 24:32.
185 Hebrews 11:1.
186 2 Corinthians 4:18.
187 ibid.

The moments of sin are nothing but moments in which we have lost the foundation of meditation or its general spirit. David in his famous sin meditated on God in front of him and meditated on the consequences of sin. He probably would not have fallen into it had he meditated before the time [of sin].

Our need for meditation:

Without it:

✤ We do not know the truth of ourselves; nor God, His good things and His gifts; nor others and their virtues; nor the truth of life. We are, then, as fools losing the jewels which reach our hands.

✤ We are as blind, not seeing the good things presented to us, so we do not enjoy them.

✤ We sadden the Giver. We forget Him and worship His gifts, and we believe that we are the cause of the gifts, so we obtain [false] hope for ourselves.

✤ We walk in life, blundering in an unknown path, with no aim, end, hope, nor experience. Therefore, we despair and are sorrowful.

Its benefits:

✤ The mother of searching[188]: it leads us to the knowledge of ourselves, so we obtain humility, the chief[189] of all virtues and the basis of the gifts of God.

✤ The mother of scrupulousness: [scrupulousness] in our conduct and our words, so we obtain the fear of God, without which we will not reach the boldness

---
188 Or: examination.
189 Literally: the head.

of His love.

✤ The mother of calmness, and the destroyer of anxiety, and the conductor to purity of prayer.

✤ "While we do not look at the things which are seen, but at the things which are not seen."[190] [It is] the basis of satisfaction and contentment, the source of consolation and happiness.

What rectifies meditation:

✤ Increasing daily solitary times and mental calmness[191].

✤ Talking less as much as possible.

✤ Transforming our attention and thinking about worldly trifles or evils, which do not profit spiritually, into holy meditation.

✤ Reading more meditative books and books of the fathers.

To train on it:

✤ Assign a notebook to record your meditations.

✤ Try to write down every day one of your meditations.

✤ If, at the start, a simple idea comes to you, do not think little of it, nor refuse recording it, but begin with recording, then reflections will follow.

✤ Do not turn meditation into building mansions in the air, nor into a topic of composition in which you care more about the literary method than the meaning.

Exercises for meditation:

Practice each exercise for a week successively, and it is

---

190 2 Corinthians 4:18.
191 Or: psychological calmness.

preferred that you seek your spiritual father's guidance.

✤ Meditate every day on one of the Creator's creations, like the inanimate, plants, animals, constellations. Enumerate some of what you notice of the manifestations of the greatness and depth of God's wealth and His wisdom.

✤ Meditate every day on one of the things that are made, that is, new things which the hand of man shaped from natural materials, like bread, buildings, cars, or any other thing of the thousands you set eyes on in any place. Write a meditation on the detailed greatness of the Creator's order of things, and the wisdom which God gave man to invent new things, using God's good things.

✤ Meditate every day on one of the contemporary incidents, whether your own incident or that of the general community, and meditate on the magnitude of God's wisdom in setting in order what no man could, regardless of how great a man's intelligence is.

✤ Everything you see or think about, whether of creatures or incidents, meditate on its good sides, regardless of how much ugliness prevails in it, for you must find in it a particular beauty. Meditate on this beauty and expel every thought of the thing's flaws that comes to you. I wish that you thank God for this beauty amid ugliness, then you will find in the deadly snake a beautiful skin of which you boast and wisdom from which you can learn. It is so with thorns and rain.

✤ Meditate every day on one of the stories of the Holy Scriptures and write down your meditations, but not your interpretations.

On Meditation Part 2

There are different types of meditations:

- ✤ Meditation on the Holy Scriptures
- ✤ Meditation on the lives of the saints
- ✤ Meditation on the virtues
- ✤ Mediation on nature
- ✤ Meditation on the other world
- ✤ Meditation on God—the Holy Trinity

Each type is a topic on its own and has its own spiritual work and particular exercise.

The first type: Meditation on the Holy Scriptures:

A man reads the holy words of God and mixes these words with his spirit, and from the mixture comes out something new, or an attempt at the discovery of the existing mysteries in the words of divine inspiration, because the words are a mere cover hiding the meanings within them; or the words of divine inspiration are a spirit incarnated in words. "It is the Spirit who gives life, the flesh profits nothing." I want this spirit; the Lord of glory says, "The words that I speak to you are spirit and they are life."[192] How then do we reach this?

It is possible here to say that meditation is the illumination of the mind by the Holy Spirit so that we may understand the meaning of the Holy Scriptures, and that we may delve deeper into them by removing the outer skin, that is, the words themselves[193], and entering into the inward part, we find spirit and life within.

We must get the help of the Holy Spirit, that we may

---

192 John 6:63.
193 Literally: the skin of the words.

reach understanding, because He is the true Author of the Holy Scriptures. Therefore, deep prayer is necessary before reading. In it we say, "Open my eyes, that I may see wondrous things from Your law."[194] Or, in another way, as appeared in the prophets, "Enlighten, Lord, the eyes of Your servant to see[195], in Your light we see light[196]." We want light from the Holy Spirit so that He may illuminate our minds and our hearts.

Meditation here is done in two stages:

✢ The first stage is defined as an effort from us, to try to discover the spirit present in the books.

✢ The second stage is a gift from the Holy Spirit, uncovering, by grace, the mysteries of the books.

I must offer my heart, for God does not intrude into the heart of man, but [He] is standing at the door knocking. If a man opens, I come in and dine with him[197] and eat of the living bread[198].

This supplication also may be [effected] by a stirring from the Holy Spirit. Therefore, some of the fathers consider meditation as a gift of the Holy Spirit, outside of human effort. Therefore, meditation requires discipleship under the Holy Spirit, and requires a man not relying on himself and his own understanding. "And lean not on your own understanding."[199]

The second type: Meditation on the lives of the saints:

Words on the first type could be applied to the second

---

194 Psalms 119:18.
195 Cf. 2 Kings 6:17.
196 Psalms 36:9.
197 See Revelations 3:20.
198 See John 6:51.
199 Proverbs 3:5.

type, except that meditation on the Holy Scriptures consists in many types. There is meditation on the historical books, which is easier—and it profits as a starting point. Because the historical books include the accounts of saintly people, it is beneficial practically speaking, that we may apply it to our personal lives. Regarding the historical books, it is good that we care about the following:

✜ Meditate on the characteristics God gives to all.
✜ Meditate on the dealings of God with the saints and His dealings with the wicked.
✜ Meditate on the dealings of the saints with God.
✜ Meditate on the dealings of the saints with the righteous and wicked.

As a result, we may come out of all this with benefits for our own life. These points may not be as clear in the prophetic or poetic books, because they do not include life stories. Also, meditation on the lives of the saints is similar in a way to the meditation on the historical books, because they are [both] stories, and the four points [above] do apply.

One of the benefits of the two types [of meditations] is that they give us a practical view of how to behave as a spiritual person. Different from this are the instructional and the law books, which are essentially commandments which are not coupled with practical examples of how they may be executed.

Therefore, we may, when meditating on the books of the law and the commandments of God, couple it with the examples we remember from the accounts of the saints and the men of the Bible, so that their lives may be applied onto these commandments as a way of instruction. An example of this is 1 Samuel 16:14–23.

The Lord departed from Saul; then a distressing spirit [troubled him]; David would sing for him, and the distressing spirit from the Lord departed from him.

We note here that the distressing spirit had no power from himself to do anything but it came from the Lord; that is, the spirit received power from God over Saul, but it could not trouble him except after the Spirit of the Lord had departed from him. Therefore, the departure of the Spirit of the Lord from Saul was the beginning of giving the devil an opportunity, for Saul became as an unfortified city.

Since this distressing spirit received power from the Lord, who, then, is able to stand before this distressing spirit except God Himself? Therefore, there had to be a person on whom the Spirit of the Lord was, that he may stand between God and Saul, so that God may see him and is thereby pleased and His heart rejoices, that He may forget His wrath. Thus the wrath of God was taken away from Saul, for the sake of His love for David. The distressing spirit saw him and was afraid, not of David himself, but of the Spirit of God in David, who is able to cast out evil spirits.

When David played on the harp, Saul would become refreshed and well[200].

The secret of the power was not in the harp but in David. Therefore, the Book says of him that he was Saul's armor-bearer[201], not merely the material armor but the armor of the spirit. Also, regarding the psalms which he sang on the harp, the power was not in their words but in the spirit that was in them, because he said them in the Spirit.

---

200 See 1 Samuel 16:23.
201 See 1 Samuel 16:21.

The Difference Between Mary and Martha

There is a difference between the meeting of Martha with the Lord Christ, and that of Mary. Martha was overcome with a spirit of argumentation and discussion. But Mary had nothing except a spirit of love and gentle complaint, and was overcome by weeping—weeping out of love and also of gentle complaint.

Thus, the Lord Christ answered Martha, perfecting her faith. Mary however, when Jesus saw her weeping, He groaned in the spirit and was troubled. Jesus wept[202].

When He commanded them to take away the stone, Martha objected—as if her faith were not perfected yet—that there would be a stench for he has been dead for four days. All the while, Mary followed the Lord Christ in silence, through love, meditation and perfect submission, by perfect faith in His power.

This is the attitude of the mind that discusses and investigates, and this is the attitude of the heart, full of faith and submission, flooded with love with which all its heartbeats move.

Inquiry and discussion are answered by persuasion, but the gentle complaint of a loving heart receives nothing but the tenderness of God, His love and His tears, followed by an immediate practical answer, even to the extent of raising a putrid dead [man].

---

202 John 11:33, 35.

A Prayer of Fr. Pimen During Service

In the name of the Father and the Son and the Holy Spirit, One God. Amen.

My Lord Jesus and my beloved God, I beseech You now, You who call me to serve Your name, that You permit me to serve none other than Your name alone, without my name; and that I may strive in Your path without evil or sin; and that You may strengthen me, to be able to live for You and to labor in Your vineyard, for the salvation of Your children; and that I may nourish them with the blessings and tidings of heaven, which You dictate to me.

I offer myself to You, that You may receive me; and [I offer] my soul into Your hands, that You may use it; and [I offer] Your gifts which You gave me, that You may lead me in the luminous path which emanates from You in me, and in my heart for all, that they may come to Your light and leave the life of darkness, and that they may experience the life of grace.

As a weak, small, foolish, as a child, I straighten myself, that perhaps You will strengthen me, and be a pledge to me, help me, and guide me, and that You do not leave me to my own self nor to the philosophy of my mind and thought, but to the guidance of Your Holy Spirit.

Hear me, for I have none but You, and You are the Rich and the Enricher; You give liberally and do not reproach[203]. Amen

---

203 See James 1:5.

On Tears

It is difficult to talk about tears! Are they not a sign of the failure of words? For when the tongue is unable to express, perplexed, [then] the heart talks, so the eyes speak with the words of tears.

Who can interpret this language?

- ✤ It is a feeling, dissolved in a drop.
- ✤ It is a tongue talking with all languages! It is the language of the soul, replete with the truest feelings.
- ✤ It is the comfort of the oppressed, the homeland of the stranger, the father of the orphan, the rest of those who labor.
- ✤ It is the atonement of transgressions, the sign of penitence, the covenant of repentance.
- ✤ It is the washing of the heart, the purification of members, the healing of the ailing soul.
- ✤ It is the language of the spirit, and the prayer of the silent; the contempt for the world, the yearning for heaven, the waiting for death.

Though tears are an object of derision to those whose hearts are locked by the bond of iron feelings, if they collide with merciful hearts, they completely dissolve them.

What have we to do with the hearts of men? Is it not sufficient glory for tears that they enter the presence of the Almighty and speak before Him! "I have heard your prayer, I have seen your tears."[204] Though they fall to the earth as a contemptible thing, they are collected into the bottle of God. "Put my tears into Your bottle."[205]

Though tears may not move the hearts of the hard-

---
204 2 Kings 20:5.
205 Psalms 56:8.

hearted, they quake the doorsteps of heaven. Though they could not prevail in changing the stiffness of rulers, they can overcome the compassion of God. "Turn your eyes away from me, for they have overcome me."[206] St. Ephraim the Syrian has a beautiful saying about tears:

> Blessed is he who is observant from here. On that day, he will be found worthy of that bliss. Though it is impossible that heavenly medicines and holiness are sold, for they are priceless, tears give them to all. I wonder, who marvels not, who is not astounded, and who does not bless the multitude of Your compassions, O Savior of our souls, for You are pleased to take tears in place of Your cures! O the power of tears! Whereto have you reached? Because you enter heaven with much boldness, with no deterrence, and you receive your entreaty from the most Holy God.

What is more, O tears, how contemptible you are in the eyes of philosophers and psychologists, even making you a sign of weakness and dissociation of personality! But is it not sufficient glory for tears that the Lord blessed the eyes adorned with them? "Blessed are you who weep now."[207]

St. John Climacus says: "It [prayer] is the mother and also the daughter of tears."[208] And this is true, because tears drive us into the chambers of prayer, and there, we are entrusted with the fountains of living tears, that we may shed of them as we wish in weeping. "Oh, that my head were waters, and my eyes a fountain of tears, that I might weep day and night."[209]

---

206 Song of Songs 6:5.
207 Luke 6:21.
208 Saint John Climacus, *The Ladder of Divine Ascent*. (Boston, MA: Holy Transfiguration Monastery, 2001), 212.
209 Jeremiah 9:1.

On Faith

Faith is the most important bond tying us to God; it is the greatest gift given to men without which there is no salvation. "He who believes and is baptized will be saved; but he who does not believe will be condemned."[210] By faith we can do anything, for "Jesus said to him, 'If you can believe, all things are possible to him who believes.'"[211]

What is faith?

- ✤ It is not a feeling, sensation, nor an emotion.
- ✤ It is not a blind calling towards obscure things.
- ✤ It is not coercion of oneself to feel the presence of God and invisible things.
- ✤ It is not the use of trickery on the mind to be persuaded of salvation, justification and redemption.
- ✤ It is not an inward emotion, made up to put the soul at rest regarding what is inconceivable by the senses.
- ✤ It is not the suppression and the combating of doubts surrounding the topics which the materialistic mind does not easily accept.
- ✤ Faith is not a personal thing which a man keeps to himself, a man who excuses himself from sharing its details with all people.
- ✤ It is not your private opinion and it is not the fruit of scientific proofs.

What is faith?

- ✤ **It is the mind's confirmation of the truths of the**

---
210 Mark 16:16.
211 Mark 9:23.

faith, in acceptance and satisfaction; in submission and surrendering, with every imagination and thought. For the Holy Spirit teaches everything and reveals [everything] until He delivers [a person] to the truth. Here, the Lord Christ—glory be to Him—says: "If you would believe you would see the glory of God."[212] The man sees that all the powers of his imagination and thought, every searching, every measure, and every comparison, increases the clarity of the truths. He sees that faith has enlarged his mind, made it grow and be renewed.

The reason for all this is that these things were inspired by God, because they are things higher than our mental level; therefore, it was necessary for God to reveal them to us.

✢ **It is the acceptance of His knowledge**. [This is] according to the truths which He declared about Himself with His very own words and His terms, because of the inability of the human mind, and its insufficiency, to comprehend of its own accord anything of the truths of God. Here the Lord Christ—glory be to Him—says: "If anyone loves Me, he will keep My word; and My Father will love him."[213] "He who has My commandments and keeps them, it is he who loves Me. And he who loves Me will be loved by My Father, and I will love him and manifest Myself to him."[214]

✢ **Our knowledge of God will remain incomplete until we know Him as He is**. "For the Spirit searches all things, yes, the deep things of God."[215] "I do not pray for these alone, but also for those who will

---

212 John 11:40.
213 John 14:23.
214 John 14:21.
215 1 Corinthians 2:10.

believe in Me through their word; that they all may be one, as You, Father, are in Me, and I in You; that they also may be one in Us."[216]

The enemies of faith are the leaning on natural knowledge, fear, and doubt.

Important notes:

✟ The man who has true faith is not he who thinks that everything is possible with God, but rather, it is he who sees that it is meet to accept everything from God.

✟ He is totally sure that his prayer will not be answered! Who is this miserable [man]? It is he who prays and does not believe that he will receive an answer.

✟ God wants us to entreat Him, wishes that we coerce Him, and desires to be overcome by His compassion.

✟ Not getting what you desire often signifies that you have gotten what is better than what you desired, like a child crying to get a knife.

✟ The person distant from Christ seldom directs his thoughts towards Christ, and even the time [when he does] is without the warmth of love and without the efficacy of the heart's faith. It is done out of necessity, and in taking refuge in Him, he is like a man who takes refuge in a person distant from him and not known to him. There is no connection between them and no affinity attracting him to the person.

✟ Those blessed, however, who do not let Christ leave their mind or their heart, they live in Christ, and He becomes their air, their food, their drink, their abode, and everything to them. He becomes all in

---

216 John 17:20-21.

all in their life.

By faith, the farmer takes the grains of wheat, which are good for food for his children, and buries them in the ground. In the evening, he goes back to his home satisfied and content, because his faith tells him that soon, he will harvest, from a single grain, thirty and sixty and a hundred fold. This is man's faith in the irrational ground.

By faith, a rich man casts his money into the market, under the mercy of the law of supply and demand, because his faith tells him that soon he will withdraw this money with great profit. This is man's faith in the law of supply and demand.

By faith, a young man writes a letter, in which he entrusts all the secrets of his heart, in which he confides the contents of his heart, in which he pours the yearning of his soul, so that it flows with ink onto the sheet. He, then, throws this letter into a post office box and goes back to his house satisfied and well pleased, because his faith tells him that the post office worker will safeguard the contents of his secrets as tightly as the Sphinx and the Pyramids have guarded the secrets of the age. This is man's faith in man.

Our faith in God, however, is nothing but a trust directed on high, in a living Being, in a rational Person, in the All-wise and All-Holy, in the living God.

On Unceasing Prayer

"I will bless the Lord at all times; His praise shall continually be in my mouth."[217]

"Pray without ceasing."[218]

"Then He spoke a parable to them, that men always ought to pray and not lose heart."[219]

Unceasing prayer is a calling on the name of the Lord Jesus with the lips, the mind, and the heart, along with the formation of a mental image of His continual and constant presence, asking for His mercy through every occupation, at all times and in every place, even during sleep.

Here, a question comes to mind: Is it our duty to pray without ceasing? And is this possible?

I say to you, try to pray and raise your heart when you are putting your clothes on, [when] you are going to bed, [when] you are sitting at the table. At the beginning of the day, look up towards heaven; let not the night oppress you and do not lose half of your life in vain in that senseless sleep. Arise, split the night and snatch light from its darkness, and prayer from its stupor, and even out of your drowsiness make an exercise for godliness. Are not the dreams of our sleep often the result of the preoccupations of the day?

O you who have stood to pray, give your heart to God, your true heart with which you love, a heart burning with love, with which you love your relatives, your friends, and those who love you; in which you sense the sweetness of pure love without hypocrisy. For unceasing prayer keeps you always in the presence of

---

217 Psalm 34:1.
218 1 Thessalonians 5:17.
219 Luke 18:1.

the King.

To maintain the warmth of a little water, it does not suffice that you bring it near a fire all at once, but it ought to have a recurrent or continual connection with the fire.

Golden advice for prayer:

✟ Remain silent for a while before [starting your] prayer as the saints have said. For prayer without meditation is like an edifice[220] without pillars.

✟ Pray audibly.

✟ Change your position [of prayer], such as prostrating, standing, kneeling.

✟ Keep a designated notebook in your pocket so that you may write in it your prayer requests, what you want [for yourself] from God and for other souls for whom you are praying.

✟ Try to write down a prayer before standing before God.

✟ Choose a suitable time for prayer.

✟ Do not despair but strive for increase and growth.

✟ Do not rush in prayer. Someone has said that prayer is like musical melodies.

✟ Experience the Holy Spirit and His work in prayer.

✟ Specify your requests, pray for them insistently, and wait for the answer.

✟ Try the life of unceasing prayer.

---

220 Also: building.

PART TWO
Father Pimen's Teaching

CHAPTER THREE
His Spiritual Sayings

His Spiritual Sayings

The following are excerpts from the sayings and teachings of our beloved father, Fr. Pimen.

✣ Terrifying it is for a dead [man] to meet a living [man], or a living to meet a dead. Nothing happens, however, if a dead [man] meets another dead, or a living with a living, for they are not affected. So is the case, if a monk, who is dead to the world, meets a layperson or meets a monk who is not dead to the world, then loss or stumbling will take place.

✣ A dead [man] has no honor, no personality, nor desires. So it is with the monk; he must have no honor, no personality, nor personal desires, for he has died with Christ that he may be glorified with Him also.

✣ The monk, to succeed in the monastic path, must mortify himself.

✣ Monasticism and worship are not a craft, but a spiritual ardent love and the good choice, love and infatuation, not worthily, but God is He who has mercy. For we do not worship God out of fear of punishment, nor out of greed for wages or recompense, but we worship Him out of love and thanksgiving for His love.

✣ If we were to mortify ourselves and crucify the body with its passions and desires[221], then this would be a proof of our love for God, but not as it were a debt, lest we be unable to pay that debt.

✣ We do not mortify ourselves and torment our souls to obtain high spiritual levels, but we worship Christ out of love and thanksgiving, feeling our unworthiness for His goodness, and [remembering

---
221 See Galatians 5:24.

that] all that we attain of spiritual progress and gifts, we are granted out of His goodness.

✢ We should not slacken from striving, lest we be considered as despisers of the grace given to us and lest these gifts be subsequently taken away from us and we do not attain the righteousness of God which is by faith.

✢ Let us crucify the tongue and mortify it from idle words which are unprofitable.

✢ The place, where love is, in it God is. Wherever love is far, there God is not found, even if it were in church.

✢ Grow in the love of God. As this love increases in the heart, sin runs away.

✢ He who wants to belong to the King does not do the things of the commoners and populace; and he who chooses a rank in the heroes' war does not do the things of boys and children.

✢ If you hear [stories] of the saints, do not think it strange, but God who gave these, may give you also.

✢ These who desire the positions of the world have no share with God.

✢ Knowledge puffs up[222], so I would that we abandon that intellectual power and say with David the prophet, "I was like a beast before You. Nevertheless I am continually with You."[223] Let us, then, crucify our minds.

✢ Engage[224] God as much as you are able, at all times, even until you reach in your prayer what the Psalm

---

222 1 Corinthians 8:1.
223 Psalms 73:22–23.
224 That is, involve God in your life.

says, "I have set the Lord always before me."[225]

✤ Humility, if it reached into hell, would lift it up to the Kingdom; and pride, if it went into Paradise, would bring it down to Hades.[226]

✤ The honor of the dead is his burial, and the honor of the monk is not going out of his cell.

✤ We have Christ. Though the world immerses us in its sins, though the devil immerses us in his darkness, though we go down from the great hope to the base—we have Christ. He will lift us up, for His blood and His redemption are active in our lives and in all our circumstances.

✤ The upright spirit is the sound balance onto which I weigh all my struggles; and the pure heart is the one which sees all things in their beautiful image.

✤ Spiritual life does not proceed in a straight line, but God permits periods of abandonment, that He may test the steadfastness of the monk.

✤ Spiritual gifts are given for free by God; virtues, however, come through striving.

✤ Love and humility destroy malice and pride, and win souls to God.

✤ The person who attains[227] true humility, wins all people and wins all hearts, with the grace of our Lord Jesus Christ.

✤ Seek true humility from Christ Himself, for He is

---

225 Psalm 16:8.
226 A similar saying by Abba Zosimas: "As the fathers have said, when his humility reaches down to Hell, the humble man is raised up to the Heavens; just as, on the contrary, when pride reaches up to the Heavens, the prideful man is hurled down to Hell." *The Evergetinos* 2, Archbishop Chrysostomos and Hieromonk Patapios, trans. (Etna, CA: Center for Traditionalist Orthodox Studies, 2008), 38.
227 Also: wins.

the God of humility and the humble.

✣ Humility is the raiment of Divinity[228], but love is God Himself[229].

✣ The Holy Bible is a personal letter from God to the monk.

✣ According to a monk's strength, he lives the life of exile on earth, is not attached to anything in the world, and does not cling to anything.

✣ True love that is from God wins all, even enemies.

✣ True monasticism is a life of repentance. Monasticism is the pursuit of possessing Christ and of uniting with Him.

✣ The class of monks is a class of toilers, giving its fruit to the Church, the world, and the service. As much as possible, the monk must keep secret his inner activities, and every activity or service he offers must not be internalized.

✣ The work of monks is like the work of the angels. Every time they praise God, they are filled with longing, love and marvelous spiritual power, making them unable to stop praising, as though the love of God, the greatness of God, the beauty of God, the power of God, the mercy of God, the tenderness of God and the care of God for all, draw them, so they cannot stop praising God.

✣ Illness is beneficial for the monk if he takes it with thanksgiving, endurance and humility.

✣ The man—who is fallen in sin, who follows his instincts, who is led away with lusts of the flesh—descends and sinks down into a bestial state.

---

228 Cf. *The Ascetical Homilies of Saint Isaac the Syrian.* (Boston, MA: Holy Transfiguration Monastery, 2011), 534.
229 See 1 John 4:8.

However, the man who triumphs over his desires is raised to the angelic rank, even that he may know the depths of God.

✢ The Lord Jesus in the gentleness of His character, did not bring the thief's attention to the fact that he had made a mistake in his request when he said, "Lord, remember me when You come into Your Kingdom."[230] But He answered him kindly, "Today you will be with Me in Paradise."[231]

✢ Jesus, there is none more tender-hearted than Him. [He] does not wound, does not reproach, does not hurt, causes no pain to a soul, does not offend the honor of any. For when He desired the salvation of the Samaritan [woman,] He did not force her to confess her sins, but said to her, "Go and call your husband."

✢ The person who believes, prays and worships Christ, without possessing Christ, is not Christian yet. This is the secret of our weakness in the world and the secret of our troubles. Because we are far away from God, we do not have any strength in [spiritual] wars, as long as we do not abide in Christ.

✢ You cannot know with certainty that God is formed in you[232] unless you are rejected like Him by people.

✢ We labor exceedingly when we walk away from our Lord and we become wearied, as though we were plowing a dry land, and as though we were drinking salt water. We will never enjoy the taste of the sweet life as long as we are far away from our Lord. Strive by yourself as much as you can, fast as much as you are able, pray as much as you may, but still, you will

---

230 Luke 23:42.
231 Luke 23:43.
232 See Galatians 4:19.

not be able to reach [the goal] unless Christ works in you.

✜ The path is easy and you will find the Lord always beside you and near you. Only if you open your eyes and call Him, you will find Him with you, no matter the depth of darkness and sin you are in. He is ready to give you everything, exactly like the prodigal son.

✜ Christ offers Himself readily to everyone. Why are you embarrassed of yourself? Why are you embarrassed of your sins? The Blood of Christ forgave the sins of the whole world—all languages, all peoples, all periods of history. Would He be wearied by you yourself?! What are you with all your sins? Nothing before the Blood of Christ.

✜ My children, it is not reasonable that we buy fruits and eat their bitter outer skin, leaving the sweetness which is within. Do not say that you know the Bible and the explanations, and that you are able to converse in theology, leaving [behind] the true companionship with God and His possession of your soul.

✜ The Lord Jesus often spoke inside a boat. The boat signifies a person, and the sea signifies the world. The boat cannot move without water, but the true danger is when water goes inside the boat; for if the world entered into a person's heart, he would be subject to perdition.

✜ No one can draw another person to Christ unless he himself is completely in Christ.

PART TWO

Father Pimen's Teaching

CHAPTER FOUR

A Dialogue with Fr. Pimen

A Dialogue with Fr. Pimen

Coptic monasticism is the cradle of monasticism in the whole world. After the repute of the virtues of the monks of Egypt was spread, and especially [those living] in the region of Scetis in the fourth century AD, many pilgrims flocked from many countries of the world to visit the monks in Scetis. They roamed among the caves of the solitary monks, asking them for a word of profit, and asking them also about many things regarding the spiritual and monastic life.

They recorded all that they heard of sayings, teachings, virtues and struggles of the elders. Many of them compiled what they had recorded during their voyages to Scetis and released them in many books. Examples of these [pilgrims] are Rufinus who collected his writings in *Historia Monachorum in Aegypto*; John Cassian who collected his writings in The Institute and The Conferences; Palladius who collected his writings in The Lausiac History; and many others who preserved for us the sayings and history of our forefathers, a precious treasure for them and the generations following them.

Therefore, we saw that it was our duty to complete what those had started, so that we may preserve the sayings and teachings of our contemporary fathers. We have collected the material of this chapter from questions some monks asked Fr. Pimen during their visits to him, and his answers, as well what we found hand-written by him in his personal journal. It is perhaps the first initiative of its kind in our modern era, to record our modern monastic heritage.

A monk asked Fr. Pimen, saying, "What is unceasing prayer? And how do we acquire it?"

The elder answered saying: "Unceasing prayer which we ought to always repeat is the Jesus Prayer (Lord Jesus Christ have mercy on me a sinner; Lord Jesus help me; I love You my Lord Jesus Christ). The Jesus Prayer is famous and renowned among monks. A person could also repeat the unceasing prayer which the Spiritual Elder used to pray: 'God, turn to my help; O Lord, hasten and help me.'

"To obtain unceasing prayer, a person has to persevere in repeating it many times throughout the day and the night. If he did this, it will not leave his heart and his thought, but it will cleave to him even in his sleep also.

"A person, in his inward mind, can think of two things at the same time, but what is important is that the prayer of the heart prevails in the mind. Though I am speaking with you right now, I am inwardly occupied with prayer without ceasing.

"The Jesus Prayer terrifies the demons and they fear it very much. It guards the mind and thought from any evil trying to enter. So many thoughts arise unexpectedly in the human mind that he must fend off by the Jesus Prayer, or accept them in the name of the Lord Jesus immediately.

"I remember what Pope Kyrillos VI used to say to his children, that within a person [there is] 'a watchdog of the spirit.' As the watchdog always guards the flock from wolves and knows how to separate the thieves from the flock if it so chooses, so does the spirit have a watchdog which distinguishes between the good and bad thoughts. Therefore, we have to keep the watchdog of the spirit always occupied to block the thoughts of the enemy as soon as they attack us."

A monk asked Fr. Pimen, saying, "Has it happened to you that one day when you had too much work, you could not complete your prayer canon?"

The elder answered saying: "One day I suffered from a very high fever, and though I am a doctor, I did not know what caused it. A thought came to me that I should rest, but I said to myself that I would rather die while I am praying than die while asleep. After I finished my prayer, I felt great consolation and felt that Fr. Faltaous of the Syrians had visited me in spirit; I did not see him bodily but felt his presence with me in the inner chamber [of my cell][233]. He prayed for me that I may get better from my illness.

After I got well, I met Fr. Faltaous and he said to me, 'I visited you, my brother, I visited you,' and I said to him, 'I felt your presence and your visit, father.'"

"Tell me, father, how did you know that the one who came to you when you were ill was Fr. Faltaous, though you did not see him?"

Fr. Pimen answered saying: "The spirit is different from the body, and the dealings of the spirit greatly differ from the dealings of the body. The body is limited but the spirit is unlimited. The more the spirit becomes exalted over the body, the more it goes into dealings and deep connections with God. In turn, He grants the spirit abilities according to its strength, and the saying of the Psalm comes true, 'Out of the depths I have cried to You, O LORD.'"[234]

---

233 Arabic: *mahbasa*.
234 Psalm 130:1.

A brother came to Fr. Pimen several times complaining about a certain sin, and when he could not refrain from it, he came to him saying, "I believe I will never be able to refrain from committing the sin, and I feel that God is wearied of me because I have repeatedly committed it, and He will not accept me because I am an evil man."

When Fr. Pimen heard these words from the brother, he said to him: "My son, do not cut off your hope in God because His mercies are superabundant. If your garment has a tear, would you repair and sew it, or throw it away?"[235]

The brother answered, "Of course, I would repair it again."

The elder, then added, saying, "There is to a mother, a son. This son insults his mother. As he is walking, he falls in the mud. Would not this mother run to him, and lift him up out of the mud [even] before he cries out to her? Have you seen a mother become wearied of her son? For if you have pity on your torn garment, and if the mother has pity on her son who has fallen in the mud and does not leave him, will God not have pity on you, and not leave you when you have fallen? He waits eagerly for your coming back to Him again; He wants you because you are His beloved son."

The brother went his way after the elder, the physician, had given him an injection of hope. From that time on he became a strong struggler, and with God's grace, he triumphed over the sin.

Fr. Pimen was accustomed to shutting himself inside his

---

[235] See *The Sayings of the Desert Fathers: The Systematic Collection*, Baker B., trans. (Florence, AZ: SAGOM Press, 2019), 290.

cell throughout the span of the Holy Great Fast, and not leaving it except on the last Friday of the fast. The fathers used to speak to him in banter saying, "We know that the last Friday of the Fast has come when we see Fr. Pimen coming out of his seclusion." Then one of the fathers asked him, saying, "How did you, father, reach this great (high) measure?"

Fr. Pimen answered him and said to him: "I did not begin the constant seclusion during the span of the Fast all at once, but gradually. I tried a two-day seclusion per week, then I added after that another day to them and so on until I progressed to the seclusion throughout the whole span of the fasts."

Then another asked him, "If someone comes to you in dire need during the times of your seclusion, would you open [your door] to him?"

The elder answered saying: "I have to open to him, meet him with all joy and love, and sit with him, for the monk has to be moderate in everything. As Abba Pimen the Solitary said, 'We were not taught to shut the wooden door but rather the door of the tongue.'"[236]

A brother from the world came to visit Fr. Pimen and said to him, "How fortunate you are, father, that you are living in the places of the saints!"

The elder answered him saying: "It is not important that we are dwelling in the places of the saints, but rather that a person carves for himself a path in the rocks."

---

236 *Give Me a Word: The Alphabetical Sayings of the Desert Fathers*, Wortley J., trans. (Yonkers, NY: SVS Press, 2014), Poemen 58.

Tell me, father, what is the meaning of the biblical saying, "Grow in the grace?"[237]

Fr. Pimen answered saying: "This means that we are still little and have not yet arrived. But there is a long way in front of us 'to the stature of the fullness of Christ.'[238] We have to understand that this is the truth, and not literature or fiction or sublimity for the mere expression. Otherwise, it is not faith. We grow in what then? In the grace which He gave us. This grace is not so that we take and then rejoice, and are happy and sleep, and we say we have arrived. No, it is a talent with which we have to trade and make profit. Therefore, he says, 'Add to your faith virtue, to virtue knowledge.'"[239]

A monk asked Fr. Pimen saying, "How does a monk die to the world?"

The elder answered saying: "The monk dies to the world when he preserves himself and his thoughts apart from the world, whether in his cell or outside it for necessary work. Also, he must not go out of his cell, like the dead man who does not go out of his tomb. For the honor of the dead is his burial, and the honor of the monk is him not leaving his cell. Finally, he must not pay much attention to the disturbance of the environment wherein he lives, nor by the noise outside his cell."

A monk asked Fr. Pimen saying, "Is it sufficient for a monk to have non-experiential[240] *knowledge of the*

---

237 2 Peter 3:18.
238 Ephesians 4:13.
239 2 Peter 1:5.
240 Or: non-practical.

mysteries of the monastic way, so that he may walk alone in the way without guidance, or so that he may express his opinion on high spiritual matters?"

The elder answered saying: "It is not sufficient that a monk knows the mysteries of the monastic way non-experientially, but he has to test it out and seek the guidance of an experienced monk who can accompany him and lead him in the monastic way.

"As to the ability of a monk to express opinion on high spiritual matters while he is still a beginner in his spiritual life and still falls into sin, this puts the monk in danger of becoming puffed up, proud and deceived by himself, [thereby] forgetting the truth of his weakness. Since he is still overcome by his sins, how can he, while still sinning, progress in the high degrees of the [spiritual] path, which are spiritual revelations and hearing the voice of God in the heart, and son on?"

A monk asked Fr. Pimen saying, "Reveal to me, father, the steps which a monk passes through in the monastic path?"

The elder answered saying: "The spiritual path always begins with fervor of spirit and immoderation. The struggle is sweet with constant victory and continual joy, and the person tastes the consolations of heaven, those of revelations, dreams, and voices of angels, with grace poured from heaven profusely. His prayer is fervent with rejoicing and hunger for more.

"This is followed by a period of testing. The disciplinary grace begins proving his conduct in the spiritual path. Grace begins to abandon him and leave him alone, that he does not find the former sweetness, nor does he feel the heavenly [things] nor the first eagerness and encouragement. Heaven is still before him, and here the truth of the soul is revealed, without the first encouragement or the early help.

"At that time, the person must proceed with perfect faithfulness and must continue in completing his [monastic] canons. His thoughts should be pure and chaste though the motives are absent, and he ought to walk by faith amidst the darkness, not looking at the present state of dryness.

"Thus, if his soul is trained on walking in the path when grace abandons him and in the times when it does not bear him, then he enters, by God's grace, into [a state of] permanent fervor and of gushing grace from heaven. The passions subside and he begins neglecting the things of the body and his minute actions (the calculated or balanced), and perhaps others would rebuke him, so this gives him humility. However, if he becomes lukewarm or prideful afterwards, some of the passions will come back to him."

"Father, your reverence told me that for a monk to succeed in the monastic way, he must mortify himself. So, how does a monk mortify himself?"

Fr. Pimen answered saying: "The monk must mortify himself, that is, mortify his carnal[241], his psychological, and his spiritual desires."

Then he came back and asked him again, "And what are the carnal, psychological and spiritual desires, to which he must die?"

---

241 Also: bodily.

Fr. Pimen added saying: "As to the carnal desires to which he must die, they are 'the lust of the flesh, the lust of the eyes, and the pride of life'[242] which is all that is in the world. He must humble his body but with wisdom, submit his body to the spirit, and must train [himself] to doing that.

"As to the psychological desires which he must mortify, they are the love of grandeur and authority, confidence in one's opinion, and holding on to the thoughts that are not related to the essence of God.

"As to the spiritual desires which he must mortify, it means that he must not unbridle his spiritual desires[243], that is, [to insist on] following a specific manner of life in his monastic way, because this is left to the directives of God in his life which he receives through his elder[244], to whom he has entrusted his soul."

A monk asked Fr. Pimen saying, "What does the Apostle Paul mean in his saying, 'I have been crucified with Christ; it is no longer I who live, but Christ lives in me?'"[245]

The elder answered saying: "You should know [something] first about life and death, for death is of two kinds.

"The first [kind] is death toward God and spiritual life, and this accompanies the life that is according to the flesh; that is, a person lives according to the passions and lusts of sin, with an unenlightened mind, even darkened towards eternal life, and [with] a will that is

---

242 1 John 2:16.
243 That is, spiritual aspirations.
244 Literally: guide.
245 Galatians 2:20.

in submission to the power of the enemy, even that he does what he wills not.

"As to the second kind of death, it is a death toward sin and the world, and this accompanies life which is according to the spirit; that is, a person lives with an enlightened mind through the knowledge of God and the desires of eternal life, being with Christ, and [with] a will in submission to the work of the Holy Spirit, that he may progress 'from glory to glory, just as by the Spirit of the Lord.'[246]

"A person cannot live unto God and the world; that is, he is [still] under the yoke of sin and the power of the flesh and its lusts, and at the same time, he is freed from sin and the flesh and its lusts. This is impossible."

"Tell me, father, how is death from sin and the world and the lusts of the flesh and the will of the enemy, accomplished in us?"

The elder answered him saying: "This is accomplished by two important processes. The first is by us, which is through the negative striving against sin and its lusts. This brings us to the cross and the tomb, only. But the second is beyond us, through the living faith and firm hope in the work of Christ in us, that is, the death of the cross. This brings us to the resurrection, and we live in the spirit of the resurrection."

"And what is the spirit of the resurrection which, your reverence, mentioned?"

Fr. Pimen answered saying: "It is a gift from God to

---

246 2 Corinthians 3:18.

those who truly die, but [die] in the Lord. 'For if we died with Him, we shall also live with Him.'[247]

"Those who war against the passions of carnal lusts and resist sin with an evident struggle, they, in Christ, believe in the Lord's death and His resurrection. Those drew near with their struggle to the cross, and by mortifying their earthly members, from fornication and uncleanness, covetousness, envy, maliciousness, and various carnal lusts, were capable of going down into the tomb and putting to death[248] the flesh to the world and all its lusts.

"Those were worthy of completing their labors by faith; therefore, the crucifixion of their passions and lusts became a road paved to receive a complementary power from the cross of the Lord, for a perfect constant deliverance. The mortification of their members becomes a means to receive a perfect death of their members from the former sin, received by the death of our Lord Jesus Christ.

"When the person completes crucifying himself by the cross of our Lord, and [completes] the death of his flesh by the death of the Lord, he can realize a new life wherein sin is not at work with its authority, and the flesh is not at work with its passions. However, he who does not step forward by himself to crucify his passions, how will he perceive or realize the power of the crucifixion of the Lord. Also, he who does not embark upon mortifying his members, how will he perceive or realize the power and work of the death of the Lord. He who does not perceive the crucifixion of the Lord nor His death, even if he believes in them, understands them and is capable of explaining them well, how will he perceive a risen life after crucifixion and death?!

---

247 2 Timothy 2:11.
248 Or: mortifying.

"Therefore, the work from our end is very important in order that we may enter the field of perception of the Lord's work which begins with sufferings and crucifixion and ends with death and resurrection! It is He who makes our faith work in us, completing everything lacking in our work and what our power is incapable of completing."

"Father, you have said in your previous answer that the person who completes the crucifixion of himself by the cross of our Lord, and the death of his flesh by the death of our Lord, he is enabled to realize the new life which is without sin. So, what is the difference between the crucifixion and death?"

Fr. Pimen answered him saying: "Death is different from crucifixion. Crucifixion is the bringing into subjection every erroneous movement in me, whether in thought, speech, or deed; and is the keeping watch for it as soon as it comes, with a ready will, and with mental and conscientious resistance, and with striving even unto loss and bloodshed.

"As to the death of the members, it is the completion of the crucifixion. That is, I preserve all the members and the body, and also the thought, away from the movement of sin, even until they seem as it were dead to sin. But [remain] watchful lest it comes back to working and life."

"Tell me, father, how does a person realize the new life?"

Fr. Pimen answered him saying: "After a person accomplishes the death of his members by the power of the Lord's death, and as a result of crucifixion and death, the person perceives the perfect power of the cross in his desires and passions, and the perfect power of death in his carnal members. Thus, by the cross, the curse, which was issued to me, was paid off; and by death, the sentence of justice was accomplished. Thus, we became innocent from the curse, reconciled with justice, capable of receiving a blessing and mercy instead of curse and justice. I find that all that concerns me as a man, as a son of Adam, has died and its power loosened. In its place, a new man arose in me, capable of living a new life with excellent spiritual abilities unlike the former, worthy of uniting with Christ fully. So I unite, and thus Christ is in me, and my life then functions in Christ who is in me, and I could say, 'I have been crucified with Christ; it is no longer I who live, but Christ lives in me.'[249]

"Therefore, we obtain new views and thoughts, truly marvelous, concerning our relationship with God and our spiritual abilities: We became temples of God[250]; we became members of the body of Christ, of His flesh and His bones[251]; we became all one body and our head is Christ[252]; we became all one body, a virgin betrothed to Christ[253]; we became His holy Church[254]; we are a living body offered by the Son to the Father; we became a dwelling of the Father and the Son together[255]."

A monk asked Fr. Pimen saying, "Is the labor of mortification, which a monk performs on earth, sufficient

---

249 Galatians 2:20.
250 See 2 Corinthians 6:16.
251 See Ephesians 5:30.
252 See Romans 12:5 and Ephesians 5:23.
253 See 2 Corinthians 11:2.
254 See Colossians 1:18, Ephesians 5:27.
255 See John 14:23.

for his salvation?"

The elder answered him saying: "All the labors of mortification which a monk performs on earth are not sufficient for his salvation, because we are not saved by the law of works but by the law of faith[256]. For though we do all righteousness, we are still unprofitable servants, because we have done what we were commanded to do[257]. But the righteousness which God gives us by faith in His only begotten Son, our Lord Jesus Christ, this is what saves us. This needs from us a struggle, that we may believe with the heart, so that this might be accounted to us for righteousness, as Abraham believed God, and it was accounted to him for righteousness[258]. Afterwards, works are required of us which are as the fruit of faith.

On the last day, if we draw near to God by our works to enter the Kingdom, then we will hear the voice that says, 'Depart from Me, you who practice lawlessness!' [259]

But if we draw near to God in brokenness [of heart] and ignominy as though we had done nothing [good], then He justifies us saying, 'Come, you blessed of My Father!'[260]

It was told of a monk who saw in a dream that his soul was, as though, taken to the place of judgement, so he said, 'Remember Lord my toil and works.' The Lord then said to the angels, 'Cut his tongue off and cast him out.'"

A monk visited Fr. Pimen and said to him, "Tell me,

---

256 See Romans 3:27.
257 See Luke 17:10.
258 See Romans 4:3.
259 See Matthew 7:23; Romans 3:27.
260 Matthew 25:34.

father, what do I do, for whenever I stand for prayer, my thoughts wander into many matters, and the enemy incites me to not pray?"

Fr. Pimen answered him saying: "Gaining victory over distraction in prayer, and what the fathers call wandering of thoughts, is not an easy thing. This is not only [a problem] for beginners in the spiritual life. Even though it is a fault, it does not, however, prevent prayer, for St. Isaac said, 'Let us remain steadfast in the prayer which is distracted until we are given prayer which is without distraction.' Therefore, do not be sad if your thoughts wander during prayer, and as time passes, they will be purified from wandering of thoughts until you reach pure prayer, devoid of wandering.

"St. Isaac also said, 'If you are waiting [to reach] pure prayer before you start praying, you will never pray then, because purity of prayer comes through prayer.' By praying for it, and from the prolonged practice of prayer itself, the mind remains steadfast in divine matters and stays away from wandering.

"Therefore, do not, my brother, ask for the degree of perfection at the starting point. For every spiritual work may begin incomplete, distorted and faulty, or at least imperfect, but by persisting in it, it is purified and uplifted, becoming perfect."

A brother asked Fr. Pimen saying, "How do we love all and stay away from all, all the while we are brothers living [together] in a monastic community?"

Fr. Pimen answered him saying: "The fundamental

and sound principle in communal life and monastic life is that I live deeply with God and have with Him a relationship and living fellowship. As an example, Hannah the mother of Samuel, what did she do when she stood for prayer?! She shook heaven, spoke with God, entered into the deep, and stood praying that even Eli thought that she was drunk. She was drunk with divine love, with a deep connection between her and God. She entered the field of marvelous divine matters. Though she did not take anything from the Lord, not a promise, not a word, nothing, she left exceedingly happy and was certain in her heart that she would receive what she wanted.

"We are brothers, and because 'the ego[261]' is still alive in us, we must resist it unto death. Though we are completely victorious over it, we must abandon it altogether. For if we do not mortify our bodies and ourselves, we will not know Christ nor attain salvation. A golden advice to all who live in a community: that I am very deep with God, superficial with people, and utterly beware familiarity. Familiarity, excessive friendship and the removal of formalities—these bring about problems and dissipate the mind without our feeling it. We have left the world. Let us then leave the manners of the world too. Thus, I am deep with God, superficial with people, and pray for all."

Then he asked him also, "How do we have one mind and one heart though we are different in character and age?"

Fr. Pimen answered him saying: "Difference in thought is not a sin but we should not lose or hate one another. Rather, [we should] understand [each other] with love

---

261 Also: the self.

and good-natured dialogue. This existed from the time of the fathers the Apostles. The Apostle Paul was going to preach in a place and did not want to take Mark with him and disagreed with the Apostle Barnabas. This ended by Barnabas and Mark going to a place while Paul took Silas and went to another place[262].

"Having differences is natural but mutual understanding is required, without it having effect on our relationship and our love towards each other. We do not want 'the self' to emerge, that is, 'my own word must be followed, I must have personality and must… and must.' Here lies the mistake because he, who does this, has the spirit of the devil of the self, within, but he who humbles himself and yields his opinion—here the outcome is good.

"In the book of Acts, it says, 'They ate their food with gladness and simplicity of heart.' [263] They sold all their belongings and placed it at the feet of the Apostles. Here is simplicity and victory over the self.

There must be temptations but, by the grace of God, we are able to walk in the way and reach [our destination]. If the other side does not accept dialogue, leave him and pray for him, and try to find another way through the intervention of the spiritual guide."

"Tell me, father, what are the degrees of purity of heart and how do I acquire it?"

Fr. Pimen answered him saying: "There is no such thing as degrees of purity of heart. We are walking in spiritual life and all virtues grow together. We strive for the sake of Christ and our goal is Christ Himself. Our goal is

---
262 Acts 15.
263 Acts 2:46.

not purity or virtue or any spiritual degree that we may attain. But our goal is Christ.

"If you want to know where you are [on the path] of purity of heart, ask yourself, 'Where am I from Christ? What extent and what distance?'

"If the life of a person were completely far away from our Lord, it would have no heart in it from the start. He is dry, empty, and he would have wasted his whole life, because our Lord Jesus is the one who fills the heart with love, consolation and strong faith, and is the one who also gives whatever we want."

"Tell me, father, how do I enter into the depth of Midnight Praises? For often I feel that it is a routine!"

Fr. Pimen answered him saying: "If we said that Midnight Praises were a routine, the praise of the angels in heaven who at all-time say, 'Holy, Holy, Holy,' would also be routine. The angels are never bored nor wearied of praise, for every time they participate in praising, their love for Christ increases in intensity. Every time they say, 'Holy, Holy, Holy,' is a new praise.

"The Lord Christ is the air for us, the essential food for the spirit and body, without whom we could never live. Midnight Praises then is not a routine—never!—but every time it gives [us] invisible power in the spiritual heart. Though the person does not understand the meaning or prays inattentively, the devils hear, run away and cannot linger around.

"Praise is the most splendid kind of prayer because in it we glorify God. For in it, we do not say, 'God give me health,' or 'prepare for me a [good] future,' or 'give me victory over the enemy.' Rather, I ask in it for God Himself and I glorify Him, and I ascend to very high degrees and join the cherubim and the seraphim. This is praise. Prayer and praise are essential things in our life."

"Tell me, father, how can a monk be earnest[264] in his life and in his relationships with those around him?"

Fr. Pimen answered him saying: "The difference between us and the great saints is that they took life earnestly from the start and did not backslide nor did they grow negligent.

"Abba Anthony left his town and crossed the Nile [river]. At another stage [of his life], he went into the inner wilderness, reaching [a place] near the sea. We do not hear that Abba Anthony went back to the world or saw his sister, or met his friends in church or service. Rather, he walked in the way earnestly.

"So, the difference between us and these saints is that they walked [in the way] earnestly, and lived earnestly, so they attained high degrees in a short time. We should not be negligent but walk in the path earnestly, in our prayers and struggles and our resistance of the flesh and ego[265], so that we may attain high degrees. It is said in the book of Revelation, 'I could wish you were cold or hot. So then, because you are lukewarm, and neither cold nor hot, I will vomit you out of My mouth.'[266]

"The person then who does not walk earnestly, will not taste the sweetness of God! Why do we [let ourselves] reach this degree, [that is,] I wish you were cold or hot? Return again and quickly. Earnestness in the spiritual life brings us directly into the depth with God."

---

264 Also: serious.
265 Also: self.
266 Revelations 3:15–16.

A monk asked Fr. Pimen saying, "How does a monk attain the love of God quickly?"

Fr. Pimen answered him saying: "I do not agree to the word 'quickly.' If we are steadfast with God, no matter what the degree of our relationship with God is, we will attain the love of God. He who desires to walk in a sound way with God, puts for himself a program within the limits of his abilities, without excessive ambition, nor lower than his abilities. For if he continues on this program, our Lord will make him grow[267]. What is important is that he walks on it earnestly, a step by step, and a stone on a stone.

"The person who walks quickly is unrealistic. God has [prepared] a special way for each one, He knows our abilities, He knows what is good for us and what is harmful, and He gives the increase.

"We ought to be at much ease that our Lord Jesus loves us under all conditions, and we should not be preoccupied with speed so long as we have surrendered ourselves in His hands.

"The greatest virtue in Christianity according to Abba Anthony is the virtue of perseverance. What is important is that we should not fall into a relapse, but walk according to our ability and we will reach, with the grace of Christ, high spiritual degrees."

A monk asked Fr. Pimen saying, "What are the conditions for discipleship under a spiritual father and guide?"

Fr. Pimen answered him saying: "There are no conditions. The main thing is that I forsake and abolish my ego from the first step in the monastic path. I ought to forsake all that I have read in books and what I have

---

267 Also: our Lord will give him the increase.

heard in sermons, and I start upon a new foundation according to the words of the elder[268] or father of confession.

"I ought to listen to guidance with humility as though it were the voice of God and it were of God's direction, [and] I ought to not cling to my opinion, because the spiritual life in monasticism is not science, psychology, nor philosophy. Rather, it is experiences we go through and receive from the saintly fathers. Monasticism has experiences and many mysteries; therefore we must follow the footsteps of experienced people. As we have learned from the saintly fathers, you should not reveal your thoughts except to the one who could cure them, because the like of these are physicians and have experience from God. Our Lord intervenes for the sake of the faithfulness of the confessor, [providing] the right guidance.

"Confession is not merely a meeting between the father of confession and the confessor; rather, the Holy Spirit is present and works between them. Therefore, beware of obstinacy, haughtiness and clinging to [your] opinion; we should rather cling to humility and perfect submission even if we possess spiritual knowledge from the Paradise [of the Holy Fathers], St. Isaac and the Spiritual Elder. All these books have contexts and are in need of clarification."

"Tell me, father, how do I cleave my mind and thought to God, [both] night and day?"

Fr. Pimen answered him saying: "We came to the monastery for the sake of God; so that we may sit with Him, we left everything. We came in order to pray, nothing more. This is our work and our main goal.

---

268 Literally: guide.

"The only place wherein we receive God is the heart, and not another place, not in Church, nor in communal gatherings, but only in the heart. In this heart, we are in solitude with God, in the inner chamber [of the cell], or on a retreat, or in the life of fellowship with God.

"The war of the monk, all his life, is a war of the thoughts, because what reveals the heart and what is therein are the thoughts. The mind or the thought is a true and clear image of the heart. Therefore, to the saints the greatest virtue is the preservation[269] of the mind.

"[For the sake of] preserving the mind, the saints struggled intensely and lived, for its sake, a very peculiar life. We learn from the life of Abba John the Short that his mind was so cleaved to God that he could not give the camel owner the things he asked for when he knocked on the door of his cell.[270] Also, how he sewed two baskets into one without realizing, from his continual preoccupation with God.[271] When the camel owner asked him about the ropes, he went into his cell but forgot [to bring them out] because he was preoccupied with things more sublime and higher; and when the man importuned him, he went in, repeating [to himself], 'The ropes for the camel owner, the ropes for the camel owner.'

"This is a true preoccupation with God, and not feigned. This is what we want to reach, but we will not reach it except through a strong relationship with God, with love, humility, and clinging to Him. Not only by struggles but also by prayer and fasting and so on. All these things are means only, and not a goal. They are only

---

269 Also: keeping.
270 *Give Me a Word: The Alphabetical Sayings of the Desert Fathers*, Wortley J., trans. (Yonkers, NY: SVS Press, 2014), John Colobos 31.
271 Ibid., John Colobos 11.

means with which we reach our goal, and subsequently we reach all of the virtues.

"The most beautiful practice in truth, in spiritual life, is the practice of unceasing prayer. The mind must cling to God and be preoccupied with Him. We ought to talk with Him about everything. This is the key to the life of unceasing prayer, to preserve the mind with Christ.

"The clinging of the mind to Christ is a very beautiful thing and very important, and it is the first and principal thing in a monk's life. Begin with any words or any matter, for whenever you have an opportunity or free time, lift up your mind and occupy yourself with Him. Talk with Him and converse with Him about some things that He may do for you or save you from; ask Him about it and importune Him time and time again, until a relationship is formed between you and Him.

"The love of Christ is the foundation of all things. The taste of spiritual struggle is beautiful and sweet because it contains hope, for God is with us, understands our hearts and feelings, and knows all of our abilities."

"Tell me, father, how do I imagine God in front of me while standing for prayer?"

Fr. Pimen answered him saying: "When I have a connection with God throughout the day, then at the end of the day, I will talk to Him not as a stranger to me, but as a person I have been with throughout the day. I will know His language and His character and His way. I will live with Him in love and I will trust that He will open His bosom with love [to me], and that He will console and encourage me. Therefore, no one should ask that he imagines the Lord Christ in front of him in a tangible physical image, because with this, he gives an opportunity to the devil, which may lead him to perdition.

"Likewise, it was said in the Paradise that the devil appeared to a monk in the form of the Lord Christ in a vision. The monk said to him, 'I do not desire to see Christ here.'[272]

"I know of contemporary fathers and saints, to whom God offered and gave gifts, but they asked God to take [the gifts] away so that they may not distract them nor make them lose humility. I wish that we walk with God in humility, and He Himself will give us true blessings."

A monk asked Fr. Pimen saying, "How is a person stripped of possessions and of the old man?"

Fr. Pimen answered him saying: "The monk ought to abandon all possessions, because he has died to the world, and ought to live a spiritual life whose goal, and all that is therein, is Christ. St. John Chrysostom says, 'If you gave a baby possessions of gold and much money, he would not care about them all because he is looking up to his mother's chest.' 'For what profit is it to a man if he gains the whole world, and is himself destroyed or lost?'[273] We should not forsake these simple commandments, feeling that we are greater than these things, but they must remain fundamental even to the end. We must be content with the bare necessities only.

"As to being stripped of the old man[274], it is [achieved] by a continual life of repentance. Repentance is not a single event and it is finished, but it is a life we are

---

272 *The Paradise of the Holy Fathers* 2, Budge A.W., trans. (London, UK: Chatto & Windus, 1907), 163.
273 Luke 9:25.
274 "Put off the old man" Colossians 3:9.

always living. Whenever we ask God for spiritual eyes, our perception[275] is enlightened and we discover new other things, against which we begin struggling to get rid of them. St. Paul the Apostle says, 'Even though our outward man is perishing, yet the inward man is being renewed day by day.'[276] Repentance then is a life wherein we constantly ask God to reveal to us what is within us.

"The most beautiful plea in the Agpeya is: 'Create in me a clean heart, O God, and renew a steadfast spirit within me.'[277] The steadfast[278] spirit is a sound balance onto which I weigh all my struggles, and the pure heart is the one which sees all things in their beautiful image and keeps away from evil [things]. So, the pure eyes and the clean pure heart sense the evil things as soon as they come in, as something foreign to them. For when we attack the devil from the beginning of the road, by the grace of our Lord, we will gain victory over him, and the Lord will put him to shame and cast him away from us."

A monk asked Fr. Pimen saying, "What is humility?"

Fr. Pimen answered him saying: "Humility in its original meaning is that a person possesses something worthy of praise yet he sees himself that he is the lowest of all people. This is like one of the saints who received from God many gifts in his spiritual life, but he considered himself the most contemptible of people and the chief of sinners. This is humility.

"Therefore, when the Master Christ willed to become incarnate, He waited until the fullness of time had come, and he found a woman full of humility,

---

275 Also: understanding.
276 2 Corinthians 4:16.
277 Psalms 51:10.
278 Also: upright.

[capable of] bearing the greatness of the gift she was to receive by the incarnation of her. The Virgin Lady is a great saint throughout the world, who received gifts no other person has received. The angel said to her, 'The Holy Spirit will come upon you, and the power of the Highest will overshadow you; therefore, also, that Holy One who is to be born will be called the Son of God.'[279] Yet she said to the angel, 'Behold, the maidservant of the Lord!'[280] This is humility and for the sake of this she received many blessings and beatifications.

"Where are we from humility? Humility is the raiment of Divinity! When a person looks at his life, his mistakes, and his weaknesses, he says, 'Where am I from humility?' Whenever he sees himself as lower than everyone, and like a little child [sitting] at the feet of Christ asking Him all that he desires and he [thinks that he] is unworthy, this is humility.

"For if humility descended to hell, it would lift it[281] up to the Kingdom; and if pride were lifted up even to Paradise, it would cause it[282] to fall down to hell."

Glory be to God. Amen.

---

279 Luke 1:35.
280 Luke 1:38.
281 Hell.
282 Paradise.

With Pope Shenouda III during making Myron

During the Divine Liturgy

With Bishop Theophilus, during Liturgy of the Water

During the celebration of Bishop Mettaos' enthronement

Lighting a vigil lamp

With Bishop Mettaos

With Bishop Kyrillos Abba Mina

With the late Hegumen Faltaous of the monastery of the Syrians

With the late Hegumen Athanasius of the monastery of the Syrians

With the late Fr. Jacob of Abba Pishoy

With some of the fathers of the monastery

In the clinic of the monastery

He has compassion on animals

He put spices on the relics of the martyr St. George

The side of Fr. Pimen's cell beloved to his heart

During Fr. Pimen's funeral

www.ingramcontent.com/pod-product-compliance
Lightning Source LLC
Chambersburg PA
CBHW031626160426
43196CB00006B/295